THE TCP/IP COMPANION

Computer Books from QED

The TCP/IP Companion

A Guide for the Common User

Martin R. Arick, Ph.D

Anura Gurugé —*Series Technical Editor & Consultant*

QED Publishing Group
Boston • London • Toronto

Anuru Gurugé — *Series Technical Editor & Consultant*

© 1993 QED Publishing Group
P.O. Box 812070
Wellesley, MA   02181-0013

QED Publishing Group is a division of QED Information Sciences, Inc.

Library of Congress Catalog Number: 93-18979
International Standard Book Number: 0-89435-466-3

Printed in the United States of America
93 94 95   10 9 8 7 6 5 4 3 2 1

Library of Congress Cataloging-In-Publication Data

Arick, Martin.
        The TCP/IP Companion: A Guide for the Common User /
        Martin R. Arick.
                p.   cm.
        Includes bibliographical references and index.
        ISBN 0-89435-466-3 :
        1. TCP/IP (Computer network protocol) 2. Computer network
        protocols. I. Title.
        TK5105.55.A75 1993
        004.6--dc20   93-18979
                                                               CIP

Contents

List of Figures

List of Tables

Foreword

The most widely used protocol in use today is TCP/IP. Nearly every UNIX system supports it, and most non-UNIX systems can support TCP/IP. Also, it is no longer an alien networking scheme for IBM, or for IBM customers. Though still rightly perceived as a worthy competitor, and a genuine threat, to IBM's own SNA and APPN networking methodologies, IBM of late, has embraced TCP/IP wholeheartedly and unreservedly. TCP/IP is now readily available on all of IBM's so-called strategic platforms from IBM itself, as opposed to third-parties, with VSE, the perennial favorite in Europe, being the only noteworthy exception. The new relationship between TCP/IP and IBM is now complementary and possible even symbiotic.

IBM's on-going rapport with TCP/IP is but just one facet of a much more open, non-proprietary and multiprotocol IBM. Spurred by competitive pressure, profoundly humbled by cataclysmic financial woes, and reenergized by a perceptive and incisive networking blueprint. IBM over the last two years has vastly broadened its outlook relative to non-IBM technology. In 1994, IBM's flagship Operating System, MVS/ESA, will support native POSIX applications. POSIX applications are typically written for UNIX systems. A new version of MVS/ESA, referred to as MVS/ESA Open Edition, will make standard, unmodified POSIX applications MVS compatible. The POSIX applications running on MVS will more than likely use TCP/IP for their networking needs. What is exciting and intriguing is the possibility of transparently integrating OpenEdition MVS with AnyNet/MVS. Now, one could have a standard, TCP/IP-based POSIX application interacting across a traditional SNA network.

Networking and computing have indeed come a long way and finally leapt over the barrier that branded applications or networks as being this or the other. With offerings like AnyNet and OpenEdition, IBM is taking a lead in paving the way towards a brave new, open world of mix-and-match networking, and consequently computing. TCP/IP, with a huge and loyal following, will be a key networking component of this world.

With the essentially seamless merging of the IBM and TCP/IP worlds, it is now imperative that IBM users have a detailed and informative reference guide as to what TCP/IP is and what it can offer. Armed with such information, IBM users will be able to exploit all aspects of the TCP/IP-oriented solutions now pouring forth from IBM. This is exactly what Martin Arick's *The TCP/IP Companion* provides. It is, however, by no way restricted to just IBM customers. It is a comprehensive and up-to-date guide that will be of enormous use and interest to any TCP/IP user-potential, as well as seasoned. The rationale for including this book in the *QED Networking Library* is the current paucity of overall TCP/IP expertise, knowledge and experience across the IBM world as a whole. IBM users, acutely aware of the TCP/IP-based solutions at their disposal, want a good book on TCP/IP. Well, here it is!

Anura Gurugé

Preface

Transmission Control Protocol/Internet Protocol (TCP/IP) provides the services necessary to interconnect processors and to interconnect networks. TCP/IP is the most widely used protocol available today. Nearly every UNIX system supports it, and most other non-UNIX systems have software available for them that supports TCP/IP. The wide availability of common networking software has led to the growth of large, complex networks. From a user's point of view, TCP/IP operates at two distinct levels: (1) TCP/IP provides the common sets of rules ("protocols") to enable computer-to-computer messaging, and (2) TCP/IP provides a set of applications ("programs") that enable users to interact with remote processors. A set of protocols that work together is called a "suite" of protocols.

This book mirrors the two-level view of TCP/IP by containing two roughly equal parts. The first part begins with a description of a widely accepted model of networks (the OSI model) and then describes the various protocols of TCP/IP and how these protocols fit into the model of networking. The second part describes the application of these protocols to provide a suite of applications enabling a user to interact with remote hosts to perform a variety of distributed functions.

The first part of the book (Chapters 1 through 8) concentrates on the user-invisible parts of TCP/IP networks to provide a foundation for understanding how TCP/IP applications work. Chapter 1 describes the networking problem and what protocols TCP/IP uses to solve that problem. Chapter 2 examines the ISO model of networks to provide a framework for analyzing and discussing TCP/IP-based networks. Chapter 3 provides an overview of the TCP/IP protocols, describing what functions are provided by each of the protocols. Chapter 4 examines an example of the data link layer based on Ethernet local area networks. The various TCP/IP protocols in the Internet Protocol layer (Network layer) are described in Chapters 5 and 6, while Chapter 7 describes the User Datagram and Transmission Control Protocols (Transport layers). This first half of the book concludes at Chapter 8 with an in-depth look at some of the files that form part of the UNIX implementation of TCP/IP with a view toward administering a TCP/IP network. Thus armed with a theoretical basis of a TCP/IP network, the user can then learn to apply these services in applications. Chapters 1-8 should be read by the more technical reader who needs to understand how TCP/IP applications work.

The second part of the book (Chapters 9 through 18) concerns itself with applications that the various services of TCP/IP provide. These applications form the basis for the user to interact with the TCP/IP protocols. This half of the book is user-oriented and focuses on the "how to's" of these applications, with practical examples of their use followed by discussion of how the underlying TCP/IP services make these applications work. Each of these chapters discusses first how the user would interact with the application and use the service of the application, and second how the application operates. Thus a user can read the first part of a chapter as a "how-to" document without needing to learn the insides of a particular application. The reader who only wants to know how to use TCP/IP should start with Chapter 9.

Chapter 9 summarizes the TCP/IP application by their function. The first application discussed in Chapter 10 is the way users can "login" to a remote system and execute commands on that remote system. Chapter 11 focuses on a more general application service that allows users to "connect" to a particular server on a remote host and use the services of that server. Chapter 12 covers copying files between two hosts. Chapter 13 describes how to execute commands on a remote host without logging into that host. The first of two chapters on file transfer applications describes a simple file transfer method suitable for diskless workstations, and Chapter 15 describes a fully functional file transfer application that can perform file name services and changing of directories and a host of other file naming services as well as transferring files. Chapter 16 discusses TCP/IP services for moving messages from one user to another; this is usually called "electronic mail." Chapter 17 examines network file systems. Finally, Chapter 18 looks into a set of miscellaneous network services such as message echo, pattern printing, and so forth.

Two appendices are included at the end of the book. The first describes the process of publishing TCP/IP standards documents and how these documents are managed; it includes a listing of the titles of the current standards documents. The second appendix provides an extensive glossary of networking terms.

A Real World Internetworking Protocol: TCP/IP

During the middle to late 60s the first attempts were made to interconnect a number of computers. By the late 60s networks containing numbers of processors were formed and operational. A number of far-thinking people began working on being able to connect separate networks, to form a distributing computing system. In this period of time the Department of Defense had a need to connect many of its computers in a distributed manner that would survive a nuclear war. The Advanced Research Projects Agency sponsored the effort to create a set of hardware and software to accomplish the interconnectivity of networks, even those whose internal software was not identical. Thus ARPANET was born. The interconnectivity in ARPANET required the use of dedicated processors, called Interface Messaging Processors (IMPs), with leased point-to-point lines to connect them. A primary service offered by ARPANET was resource sharing; a researcher in one network could connect to a host in another network to use that host, which might be a supercomputer.

At the same time that ARPANET was established and growing, several other networking technologies were coming of age, such as Ethernet, Token Ring, and so forth. These technologies also used dedicated hardware and software to interconnect hosts. A new problem then arises: how to interconnect two different kinds of networks. Each of the network types uses a particular set of hardware and software to effect interconnectivity within a homogeneous network, but these sets of hardware/software are incompatible. What was needed was a set of software that operated on top of the networking methodologies and that could manage the information exchange between two different networks.

The problem that the designers of TCP/IP needed to solve is illustrated in Figure 1.1: Host A and Host B desire to exchange information with each other. Whether they are on the same physical network (as in Figure 1.2) or on different networks (as in Figure 1.3) need not be apparent to either host. In fact, only the name of the host with which to communicate should be needed.

The most basic service that is desired is based on moving information from one host to another. Thus the first part of the problem is software that will be able to move information from one host to another regardless of the networking methodology used. Furthermore, the existence of incompatible networking methodologies must be acknowledged and overcome. The first piece of this software is the Internet Protocol (IP) software, which sits on top of the networking methodologies and manages the addressing of one host to another and the fragmentation of packets due to networks having differing message sizes. But this protocol does not provide reliable data transport. Applications might want reliable data exchange, and this is added via the Transmission Control Protocol (TCP). (For applications that do not need reliable data exchange, the User Datagram Protocol is available, which is much simpler to implement but provides less services.)

To make the problem more approachable, the designers came up with several sets of services, or rules ("protocols"), that could be used by either their own applications or foreign applications. This approach led to a natural form of layering by assigning different layers different functions that need to be available for internetworking to function. Figure 1.4 enlarges on the problem shown in Figure 1.1 and adds some distinct software layers to the original view. This particular model has only five layers, while other models might have more (or less).

Figure 1.1. Model of two communicating hosts.

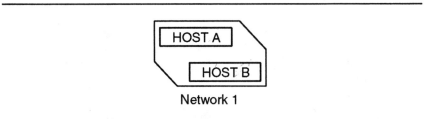

Figure 1.2. Two communicating hosts in the same network.

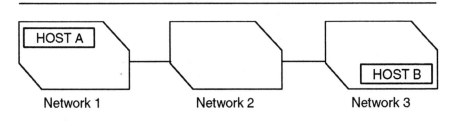

Figure 1.3. Two communicating hosts in different networks.

In Figure 1.4, the names of protocols that TCP/IP will provide in this model can be added. This group of protocols includes the Internet Protocol and the Transmission Control Protocol, as discussed previously, but in fact a number of protocols have been added to solve various problems caused by internetworking. Figure 1.5 details the major protocols that the TCP/IP suite contains.

Each of these protocols solves a particular problem that will be described in some detail in the following chapters of the first part of this book.

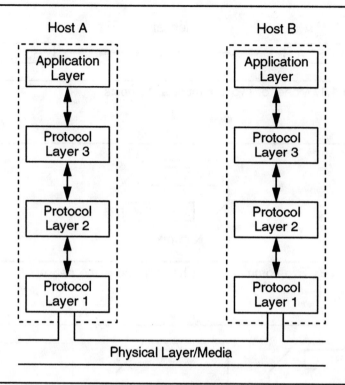

Figure 1.4. Layered model of communicating hosts.

Early designers determined that all of the three types of services were considered the minimum needed for a fully functioning internetwork: (1) mail services to exchange messages between hosts, (2) file transfer services to move files from one host to another, and (3) terminal services to allow connection and execution of commands on a host remote from a terminal. Each of these types of services is part of the TCP/IP software but uses the protocol suite itself. These applications will be discussed in the second half of the book.

After TCP/IP was created, the Defense Communication Agency mandated that all networks connected to the ARPANET use TCP/IP by January 1, 1983; thus the Internet was born.

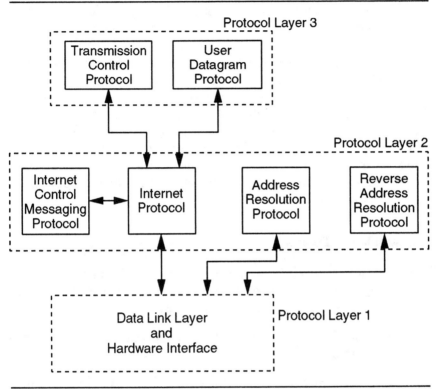

Figure 1.5. Suite of TCP/IP protocols.

These early developers of TCP/IP quickly recognized that the only methodology that could accomplish the task of wide availability would be to establish standard procedures for the functions that networks need to perform. These workers understood that these procedures need not specify how the task was to be accomplished, but only how one processor would view its interaction with the network and its interaction with other processors with which it wanted to communicate.

To promulgate these ideas and to encourage software to be written for a variety of processors and operating systems, the sponsors of TCP/IP began to publish a series of documents that would develop the basis for this internetworking methodology (available from several sources, including networks, of course). These documents, published as discussion documents to be commented on, were named "Request For Comments," or RFCs. The goal of this series of documents was to both inform (provide the basis for an internetworking protocol) and to encourage discussion of features that would be needed for internetworking capabilities. Over the years most of the original documents have been superseded by revised versions, and extensions have been added along the way. Some of these documents were just commentary on the process; others were commentary on life. The original series of documents were published in the middle to late 70s.

Networking Terms

The following is an introduction to some of the terminology that a discussion of TCP/IP involves. A more complete set of definitions are found in the glossary in Appendix B.

Protocol — a set of rules to be used between two communicating devices.

Encapsulation — the addition of control information to the data. In the layered model of networks, each successive layer does not look at the control information that the other layers have added.

Virtual circuit — a connection that is established between two application programs. To establish a connection requires a specific sequence of operations. The establishment of a "circuit" is most effective in the case where a number of messages are going to be exchanged. (In a later chapter, we will find that the TCP protocol is used to establish virtual circuits.)

Datagram — a message that is sent when no connection has been established between two communicating hosts. Each message is treated as an independent unit. (In a later chapter, we will find that the UDP protocol is used to send datagrams.)

Port number — the address of an individual application on a particular node. Port numbers less than 1024 are reserved for standard services.

Internet address — an address that the internet protocol uses to address a particular host.

Ethernet address — an address that is associated with the Ethernet hardware.

Application — program that provides end user services such as electronic mail, file transfer, or terminal connection to a remote host. These programs use the various protocols in the TCP/IP suite.

Network — a collection of processors linked together physically or logically.

Internet — a connection of two or more distinct networks.

One note on terminology: the term "internet" or "Internet" is used throughout this book to mean collections of networks and their interconnection, particularly in reference to networking protocols. In Appendix A and Appendix B references are made to an organization called "Internet" which is both an administrator of a large body of interconnected networks and a sponsor of ongoing development of TCP/IP.

2

The OSI Model of Communications Networks

Introduction

In this chapter a model of communications networks is examined that is widely known. This model, although not strictly adhered to by TCP/IP, provides a framework for a discussion of the inner workings of TCP/IP that will follow in succeeding chapters. An understanding of the model will enable us to understand why TCP/IP is constructed the way it is.

What Is the OSI Model of Communications Networks?

An interconnected set of lines and terminals allowing processing to take place in one or several locations is usually viewed as a **network**. A network may have several hosts interacting with multiples of terminals. To bring structure to this view of a network, the concept of **network architecture** is proposed, which is a structured hardware and software design that supports the interconnection of a number of physical and logical components.

A network architecture is a way to define the set of rules to which these interconnecting elements must conform. It is not, however, a definition of how the internal design is made or how the functions in the network operate or how a rule is actually implemented. A network architecture is a statement of what services need to be provided to enable the network to follow one set of rules.

In the past several years the International Organization for Standardization (ISO) has developed a model of network architecture called the Open Systems Interconnection (OSI) model of network architecture. The goal of this model is to promote the interconnecting of networks of all types.

The underlying principle exploited by the OSI model is "layering." The idea is to create a network architecture with several layers in which each layer provides certain unique functions that are not provided by any of the other layers and the interface between each layer is strictly defined. Based on some standard structuring techniques, the OSI model defines seven distinct layers, as shown in Figure 2.1. Each layer need only interact with the adjacent layers and has no knowledge about any other layers, as illustrated later in Figure 2.2. Information flows down through the layers of the sending host and then up through the layers of the receiving host. Because the layers are isolated from each other by strict interfaces, information that is added by a layer in the sending host will only be used by the matching layer in the receiving host. In this sense the matching layers of the sending and receiving hosts communicate with each other in a peer-to-peer relationship as illustrated by the dotted lines connecting matching layers shown later in Figure 2.2.

Each layer adds value to the services provided by the set of lower layers in such a manner that the highest layer is offered the set of services needed to run an application distributed over several networks. Each layer provides services to the layer above and requests services from the layer below. Thus the total network problem is divided into a set of smaller problems.

Intermediate networks that merely relay information from one network to another will only need to implement some of the lower three layers to act as transferral agents. Figures 2.3, 2.4, 2.5 and 2.6 (shown later) illustrate this principle of the OSI scheme for differing network problems.

| 7. Application Layer |
| 6. Presentation Layer |
| 5. Session Layer |
| 4. Transport Layer |
| 3. Network Layer |
| 2. Data Link Layer |
| 1. Physical Layer |

Figure 2.1. Seven layers of OSI model communications network.

The Seven Layers in the OSI Model

Each of the layers has a different unique set of functions to perform. The functions of each of the layers will be discussed.

Layer 1, the physical layer, provides the mechanical, electrical, and procedural characteristics to establish, maintain, and release physical connections between data link entities. This layer provides the physical link between devices and the network. Some of the current standards in this layer are RS-232C and RS-449. This layer sends and receives a stream of bits across the medium, providing a physical connection between two communicating systems.

Layer 2, the data link layer, provides the functional and procedural means to establish, maintain, and release data links between network entities. This layer ensures that transfers of data take place error-free on noisy channels. This layer provides error correction and sequencing. All of these functions will probably require extra information to be added to the data. Some methods add to the end of the message a checksum (where all of the bits in the message have used in some numeric calculation), which is used to test whether this message was correctly received. This layer will cause retransmission of the message if there is an error. Some of the current definitions of this layer are Ethernet and Token Ring.

Layer 3, the network layer, provides for the exchange of information between two entities over network connections. This layer allows a node-to-node type of operations in a network where intermediate systems (hosts) may only be used for moving data around. This layer is a delivery service, and layers above this will not be able to transfer information from one physical node to another physical node. This layer provides independence from routing and switching considerations for the rest of the network. This layer controls routing between nodes with no direct connection by querying intermediate nodes to determine a route between non-physically connected hosts. Thus intermediate nodes need only contain up to the network layer in order to provide message relay services.

Layer 4, the transport layer, is for the transparent transfer of data between session entities (processes) that need not worry about data transfer between each other in a cost-efficient manner. This layer is needed so that the available communications service can be optimized to provide network performance needed at a minimum cost. This layer segments messages into smaller pieces if the lower layers cannot handle the full message at one time or if it is more cost-effective to do so. This layer implements flow control so that lower layers would not be swamped with data.

Layer 5, the session layer, binds and unbinds distributed activities into relationships. Binding is the setting up of communications between two processes, and includes sending from one process to the other any necessary parameters that describe the originating process. This layer controls data exchange, synchronizes data operations between two entities, and controls the dialogue between two users. The session layer determines the way data is sent, either in one direction only, in both directions alternatively, or in both directions at the same time. This layer structures that dialogue between the two communicating systems.

Layer 6, the presentation layer, handles the representation and manipulation of data for the benefit of the application programs. This layer handles the transformation of terminal data from the "real" terminal device or application data generator into a standard terminal data stream by performing code and format translation. This "virtual terminal" concept represents all terminal functions in a standard way. In this model, the network knows only one type of terminal, the virtual terminal. Message compression and/or encryption could be done in this layer.

Layer 7, the application layer, is the highest layer and handles the management of the OSI network. This layer is responsible for collecting data concerning establishment of connections for data transfer between application processes. Not much work has been done on this layer where information processing occurs. This layer provides different services depending on what the application needs.

The OSI model forms the framework that all current and future networks will be measured against. Further, there is wide agreement that the OSI model is a needed development, and manufacturers of data communications equipment and software will work to conform to the OSI model.

When two hosts are located in the same network, this layering methodology may seem cumbersome and not necessarily providing functionality. Figure 2.2 illustrates this case of two hosts on the same network. Notice the flow of data down the different layers and then back up the different layers. The next section will examine situations that require applying these techniques in order for data to move from one host to another. For example, how do you move data from a host in one network that uses one set of protocols to a host on another network that uses another set of protocols?

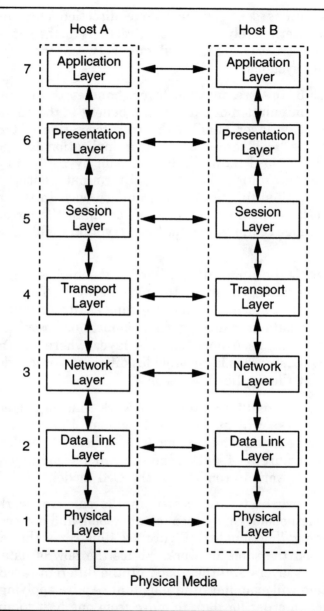

Figure 2.2. How OSI model hosts communicate on same network.

Applying the OSI Model to Two Communicating Hosts

The OSI model predicts that three different possibilities exist for enabling communications between two hosts: (1) connection through the physical layer, (2) connection through the data link layer, and (3) connection through the network layer. Which possibility is chosen will depend on the services that each of the two communicating hosts needs. Each of these three cases will be analyzed.

Suppose that the physical location of two hosts extends beyond the limitation of the physical layer characteristics (more than 1500 meters for Ethernet-based data link layers with coaxial cable). How can you then move messages from Host A to Host B? Because of the layering methodology only the contents of the physical layer would need to be moved from Network 1 to Network 2. Figure 2.3 illustrates interconnecting two hosts on different networks through a device that operates only at the physical layer level. This device need only copy the electrical signals from one network to the other and vice versa. These devices are called relays or repeaters.

Repeaters are physical layer devices that just copy electrical signals from one segment of a network to another. Repeaters are often used in local area networks to extend the network. Ethernet-based local area networks have a limited range based on the time it takes for a signal to travel to the end of the cable and back again. This length is roughly 1500 meters. If all of the network devices cannot be co-located within this distance, the network can be extended by inserting a repeater to resend the signal from one network to the other.

The second case is that the two networks are compatible down to the data link layer. For this type of interconnection, a device that operates at the data link level will be needed. Such a device is called a bridge and is shown in Figure 2.4, illustrating the case of one network that uses Token Ring as its data link layer and the other network that uses Ethernet as its data link layer.

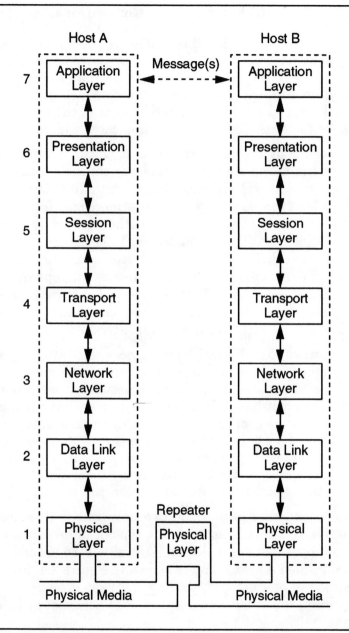

Figure 2.3. How OSI model hosts communicate through repeaters.

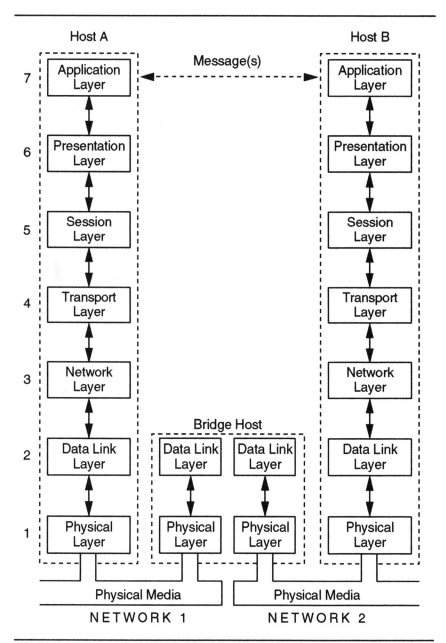

Figure 2.4. How OSI model hosts communicate through bridge hosts.

Bridges are components that connect local area network segments that are too large to be constructed as one. Bridges forward packets from one network segment to another until the segments reach the local area network that contains the host being addressed. In a network with a number of separate local area networks tied together, packets may travel through a number of bridges before finding the correct local area network. Bridges operate at the data link layer and base their filtering and forwarding decision on the hardware address of the network interface cards. As such, they are geared to handle the protocol and addressing scheme of a particular type of data link layer.

The third case is that the two networks are compatible only down to the network layer. In this case two different devices exist: gateways and routers.

Gateways are devices that interconnect two or more networks. They often perform some specific protocol conversion at layers above the network layer to move data from one type of network to another, as shown in Figure 2.5. For example, suppose two different networks want to exchange data; one network is based on Digital Equipment Corporation's DECNET protocol, and the other is based on TCP/IP protocol. A gateway can be used to move data from one network to the other. A gateway has network connections in each of the different networks that you want to connect and its job will be to move messages from one network to the other, performing whatever protocol translations are necessary.

Routers operate at the network layer and will move messages from network to network, as shown in Figure 2.6. Routers make logical decisions about the pathway through the networks. Routers usually operate on the addresses that the particular protocol provides.

Routers can be used to create a barrier between a local network and the outside world. That is to say, all the other networks that are connected to a particular network may be isolated from it except for the specific messages that are destined for hosts

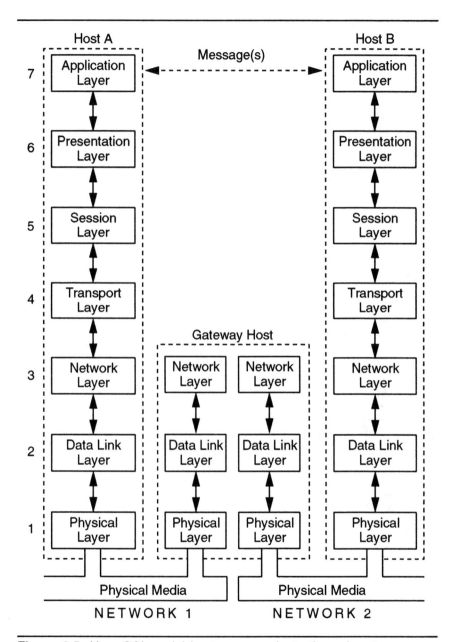

Figure 2.5. How OSI model hosts communicate through gateway.

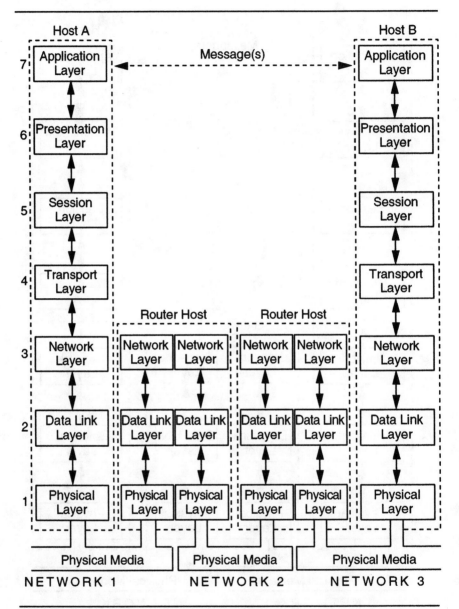

Figure 2.6. How OSI model hosts communicate through routers.

on the local network. Routers operate at the network layer and can recognize and manage protocols and multiple connections to networks. Routers need to be configured with addresses, protocols, and routes to particular hosts. Routers can usually only handle routing between networks that use the same protocol. They can route between networks that use different data link layers such as Ethernet, Token Ring, and so forth, so long as they all use the same protocol.

Summary

This chapter has examined the OSI model of networks, which proposes that there are seven different layers with different functions to adequately describe the mechanisms of moving data from one network to another. Each of these seven layers has its own distinct functions. Use of some or all of the layers may be necessary to move data from one host to another. Several cases where only some of the layers were used to move data from one host to another were illustrated.

For further study, the following papers are of interest: Gray, J. P. and T. B. McNeill, *IBM Systems Journal* 18(2) (1979): 263–297; Green, P. E., *IEEE Transactions on Communications* 28(4) (1980): 413–423; Shoch, J. F., Y. K. Dalal, D. D. Redell, and R. C. Crane, *Computer*: (August 1982) 10–27; Stallings, W., *Computing Reviews* 16(1) (1984): 3–41; and Zimmerman H., *IEEE Transactions on Communications* 28(4) (1980): 425–432.

3

Protocols of TCP/IP

Introduction

In this chapter TCP/IP is examined to see what its structure is and how it functions in light of the prior chapter on the OSI layered model of communication networks. Each of the various protocols of TCP/IP is discussed in relation to its place in a layered model of computer networking. How data moves through this layered scheme is illustrated with particular reference to the units of information that each layer processes. The services the two protocols in the transport layer provide are compared, and how these protocols are used by TELNET is illustrated.

Physical Model of a Network

For two computers to communicate with each other there must be a physical pathway between them that messages can traverse. Two different models for this physical connection are possible: the first is that the two hosts reside in the same local network, and the second is that the two hosts reside in different networks that are connected by gateways. Figure 3.1 shows these two physical models schematically.

In the first model, messages can be sent directly from one host to another without any assistance from intermediaries, but in the second model the help of at least one extra host will be necessary for a message to get from Host 1 to Host 2. TCP/IP handles both types of communications.

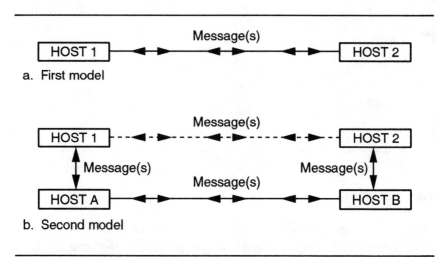

Figure 3.1. Two physical models of two communicating hosts.

For the first model, the connection between the two hosts is direct. The second model illustrates a type of connection usually called "virtual" in the sense that Host 1 and Host 2 believe that they are communicating directly with each other while in reality there is at least one and possibly several other hosts that are relaying the message. Virtual connections are shown with dashed lines to differentiate them from "real" connections. TCP/IP even provides for different routes through the network for successive messages.

The next section will illustrate how TCP/IP can accomplish both kinds of connections.

Layers of TCP/IP

If we examine TCP/IP as a layered data communications networking product, a simplified model such as Figure 3.2 would show the various layers of TCP/IP. In this diagram the name of the layer in the OSI model is shown on the left side and the main protocol that TCP/IP provides is shown on the right. This model of TCP/IP shows just five layers to the TCP/IP networking software and not seven as the ISO standard would require. TCP/IP does not follow the ISO standard because neither a presentation layer nor a session layer is individually defined. TCP/IP applications provide the services of these two layers as necessary.

Application Layer	APPLICATIONS
Transport Layer	TRANSMISSION CONTROL PROTOCOL
Network Layer	INTERNET PROTOCOL
Data Link Layer	(NETWORK INTERFACE PROTOCOLS)
Physical Layer	(PHYSICAL NETWORKS)

Figure 3.2. Model of TCP/IP layers compared with OSI model.

For the bottom two layers of the OSI model, data link layer and physical layer, TCP/IP does not provide any specific protocol but instead interfaces with whatever protocols are available.

TCP/IP is really a family of protocols, each of which is designed to solve a particular network communications problem. The view of TCP/IP layering in Figure 3.2 provides a simplified model while Figure 3.3 gives a more detailed view, again providing reference to the layers that the OSI model contains. The more detailed model illustrates that for the network layer, there are a number of protocols that TCP/IP provides; for the transport layer, there are two protocols that TCP/IP provides; and for the application layer, there are again a number of applications that TCP/IP provides. For the data link layer and the physical layer, TCP/IP provides no new protocols but instead interacts with the protocols that others provide.

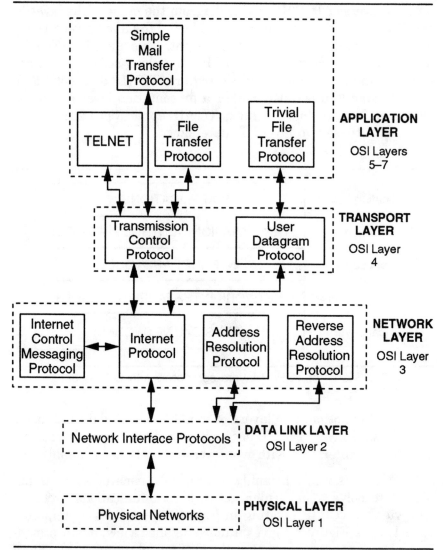

Figure 3.3. Protocols of TCP/IP.

To pass data from one computer to another, the data will move successively through the layers of the communications software system, as shown in Figure 3.4(a). Each layer performs specific functions that enable a message to move from one host through a network to another host; it adds specific information to the message, as shown later in Figure 3.5. If there are intervening hosts that must route the data through the network to another host, only the data link layer and possibly the network layer of TCP/IP in the intervening hosts are involved, as shown in Figure 3.4(b).

Each layer on the sending host adds information to the message and each layer on the receiving host removes information from the message. This process is called encapsulation. Thus the application layer will generate the data and pass that data to the transport layer. Then the transport layer on the sending host will add information to the front of the data and will pass that to the network layer. As each successive layer adds information, the message will become longer. In the receiving host, the information that was added by each layer in the sending host will be used and removed by the corresponding layer before passing the information to the next higher layer. A schematic diagram of how this works is shown in Figure 3.5.

Routing data from one application on one node to another application on another node is done via a two-layered approach. At the transport layer, the address is a "port number" (16 bits long). This is the particular identification of an application on a particular node. It is unique to the application on the node; no other application can have that port number. This is a logical connecting point for an application.

The actual node that the information is going to is specified in the next layer down, the network layer, which uses addresses that are 32 bits long and are usually called internet addresses. Each host is assigned at least one unique internet address. In the next layer down, the data link layer, the address of the receiving host is translated to a physical address and passed onto the network to be communicated to the receiving host.

In the next sections, starting with the bottom layer and moving up the layers, we will examine the information that each of these layered software protocols adds and how that information is used.

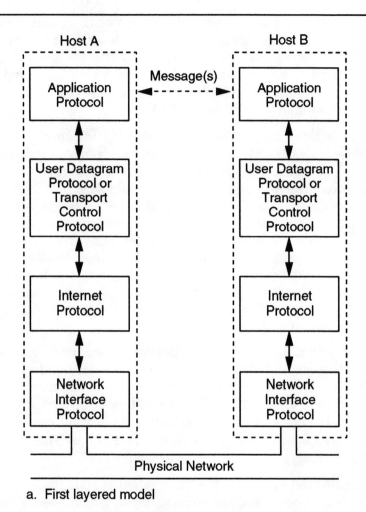

a. First layered model

Figure 3.4(a). Two layered models of two communicating hosts.

Data Link Layer of TCP/IP

The data link layer of TCP/IP can use any variety of networking systems such as Ethernet, Token Ring, and even X.25. This layer of the protocol attaches the appropriate header depending on what type of hardware/software is being used. Figure 3.5

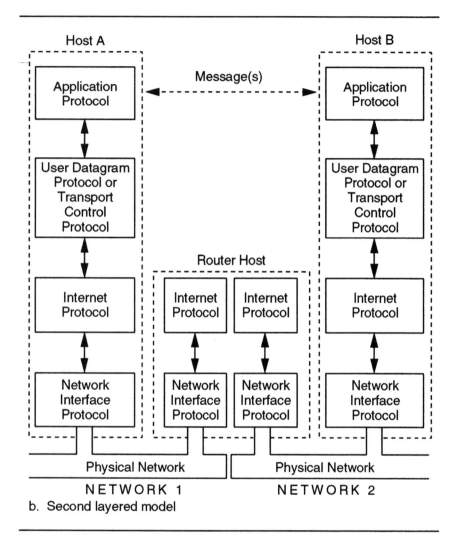

Figure 3.4(b). Two layered models of two communicating hosts. (cont'd)

illustrated how the Ethernet header (and trailer) would be added by the network layer if an Ethernet-based data link layer were being used. Similar headers would be added by other data link protocol methods. TCP/IP does not uniquely define this layer and instead uses any data link layer that provides a communications pathway from the sending host to the receiving host.

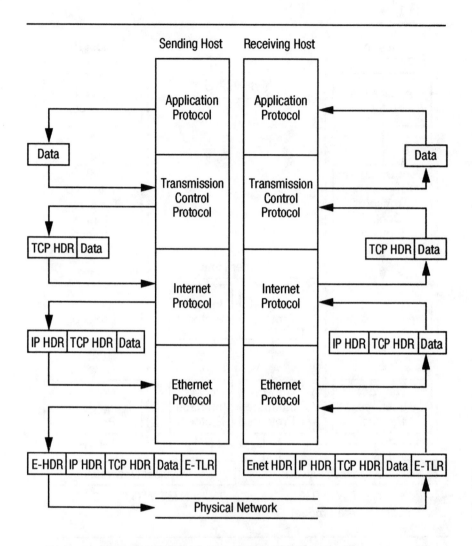

Note: "TCP HDR" is the header Transmission Control Protocol adds; "IP HDR" is the header Internet Protocol adds; "E-HDR" is the header and "E-TLR" is the trailer that the Ethernet software adds.

Figure 3.5. Transmitting a message from one host to another.

Network Layer of TCP/IP

For the network layer, OSI Layer 3, TCP/IP offers a variety of protocols, of which only the Internet Protocol (IP) offers the ability to move data between hosts. The other protocols offer special services to aid IP in its functions.

The internet protocol requires that each host in a network have a unique address, called the **internet address**. These internet addresses are registered in the */etc/hosts* file or provided by a name service. Once the internet address of a host is known, it can be sent messages using IP. The IP attaches its header as the message is passed to the lower-level protocol as shown in Figure 3.5.

The Internet Protocol layer provides several other protocols that assist the Internet Protocol itself in its task of moving messages. Address Resolution Protocol (ARP) provides a method for translating internet addresses into hardware addresses, and Reverse Address Resolution Protocol (RARP) provides a method for translating hardware addresses into internet addresses. Thus messages bound for or coming from a host whose hardware address is known or whose internet address is known can be presented to the Internet Protocol for processing, or to the data link layer for sending to the destination host. Another protocol in this layer, Internet Control Message Protocol (ICMP), provides error reporting services so that problems in delivering messages can be discovered.

Transport Layer of TCP/IP

The transport layer provides services so that one application program on a particular host can communicate with another application program on a remote host. TCP/IP provides two protocols in the transport layer: one is a nonguaranteed "datagram"-based service, which is called the User Datagram Protocol (UDP), and the other is a reliable data stream, which is called Transmission Control Protocol (TCP). These two protocols offer different services, as listed in Table 3.1. A user application can choose which of these two protocols to use depending on which set of services that application needs.

The transport layer adds the address of the service on the remote host to the data the application layer generates. This address is called the port number and can be determined for well-known services such as mail, file transfer, and so forth, by examining a file called /etc/services. This port number is specific to the type of protocol (either UDP or TCP) that is being used and must be unique to the application.

Service	UDP	TCP
Connection oriented?	N	Y
Message Boundaries?	Y	N
Data Checksum?	Optional	Y
Positive Acknowledgment?	N	Y
Timeout and Retransmit?	N	Y
Duplicate Detection?	N	Y
Sequencing?	N	Y
Flow Control?	N	Y

Table 3.1.   UDP and TCP services compared.

For specific services provided by TCP/IP-based clients, you will have to determine their "well-known port address" by examining the /etc/services file or by using one of the system services to request the port number for a particular service. For example, the ftp server uses port number 21. To send a request to the ftp server, you would address your request to port number 21 on the host of interest.

As shown in Figure 3.3, there are two protocols that can be used for the transport layer (ISO Layer 4): TCP and UDP. Thus there are two different methods for two user processes to pass data between each other. As an example of the use of one particular method, the TELNET application uses TCP as the Transport Layer Protocol, as shown in Figure 3.6. Other applications use UDP. Which of the two protocols is used in the transport layer depends on which set of services the application needs.

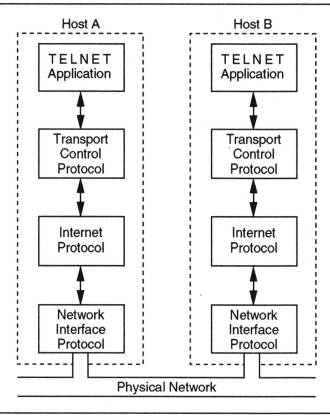

Figure 3.6. How TELNET uses TCP/IP protocols.

Application Layer of TCP/IP

The application layer of TCP/IP will appropriately format the data that is to be communicated to the receiving application layer and perform the services that are necessary. This data is then passed to the transport layer for further processing. The services provided by this layer include name services so that pathways between hosts can be determined, file transfer services so that files can be transferred between dissimilar processors, mail services so that letters can be exchanged between users, and TELNET services so that terminal devices on one hosts can interface with remote hosts. In addition, some TCP/IP implementations include remote command execution services so that commands can be executed on a host to which you are not connected.

Units of Information in Each Layer

The units of information that are handled by each of the layers in a TCP/IP network are indicated in Figure 3.7. The application

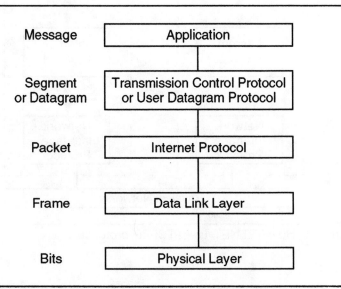

Figure 3.7. Units of information used by TCP/IP protocol layers.

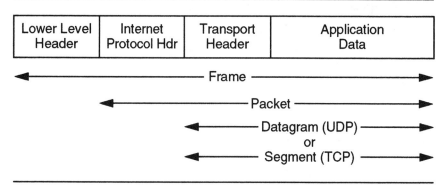

Figure 3.8. Units of information during transmission of messages.

layer creates data that it passes to the transport layer; the transport layer turns the data into messages, which it passes to the network layer. The network layer will divide the messages into standard-sized pieces called packets. Finally, the packets are broken by the data link layer into frames that are matched in size to the particular medium being used. Because TCP/IP networks pass packets between nodes of a network, these networks are often called **packet-switched networks**.

A slightly different way to examine this is illustrated by Figure 3.8, which shows how the message with all its headers is assembled by the various layers as they transmit it.

Summary

This chapter examined how the layering that TCP/IP uses is applied to the task of moving information from one host to another. References to the OSI model provide a framework for the protocols that TCP/IP provides. Each of the layers of TCP/IP, together with the variety of protocols that TCP/IP provides, are discussed in outline form. Chapters 5, 6, and 7 discuss in detail how each of the protocols in TCP/IP operate. The units of information that each layer operates on are discussed.

One quite useful source of information is an IBM publication: *Communication Concepts and Procedures for AIX Version*

3 for RISC System/6000, First Edition, March 1990, Document Number SC23-2203. It describes in general terms how TCP/IP is viewed by IBM and what facilities are part of their TCP/IP implementation.

4

Local Area Networks: Data Link Layer

Introduction

Data communication equipment that can be used to connect two devices that may be located anywhere. This kind of network connection is part of a type of network called a wide area network (WAN). In fact, whether the devices are actually quite close together or far apart has no bearing on what kind of equipment is used to connect them. But if the devices were close together, could we take advantage of that fact to provide better service?

A networking scheme exists that would take advantage of proximity of devices. In addition, this networking scheme is capable of servicing a large number of devices that are close to each other. This chapter will discuss a networking method that will be able to connect together all of these "local" devices and computers.

Characteristics of Local Area Networks

Local area networks (LANs) are different from wide area networks in several respects. First of all, there is a limitation to the separation between the devices on the network. Generally, all of the devices on the network must be within a few kilometers of each other. Second, local area networks have no central control; in fact, the devices on the network communicate peer-to-peer with each other. There are no masters or slaves in these networks. Each device on the network, called a node, has the intelligence to control its communications on the network and to share the communications media with the other devices on the network. Third, local area networks are high-speed networks with typical bandwidths of five to ten megabits per second. But this speed comes at a cost, with each connection to the local area network being substantially more expensive than simple modems. Fourth, local area networks have a built-in error detection and correction mechanism that limits the error rate to less than 1 in every 10^8 bits.

A LAN is capable of supporting several hundred devices on a single network, although some degradation in throughput will begin to be evident as more devices are attached. Every device is connected to the same "pipe" and thus can talk to any other device on the pipe. In this case the pipe is a local area network.

The medium used for local area networks is some form of coaxial cable. There are several kinds that have been used; one type of coaxial cable is about 1/2 inch across and carries signals in the 5 – 10 megahertz range. Another kind of medium is the twisted-pair media used for telephone wires. This medium has the advantages of being easy to install, inexpensive, and widely available. A serious disadvantage is that the available bandwidth is quite limited, in the range of 150 kilohertz to 1 megahertz over short distances.

Currently, several implementations of local area networks exist, and these will be examined with respect to the conditions that make them useful, how they are set up, and what their topology is. The three principal types of local area networks to examine are:

- Baseband bus

- Broadband bus

- Token Ring

We will examine these implementations one at a time.

Characteristics of a Typical Baseband Bus Network

First we will look into the baseband bus implementation of a local area network. The characteristics of this type of network are:

- Shielded coaxial cable (50 ohm)

- 1 to 10 megabit per second bandwidth

- 2.5 km maximum length of network

- Can connect up to 1024 stations

- Bus arbitration via contention

- No central control in the network

- Media is passive

Generally, the standard baseband bus network is called "Ethernet."

Topology of an Ethernet Network

The simplest topology of an Ethernet network is illustrated in Figure 4.1.

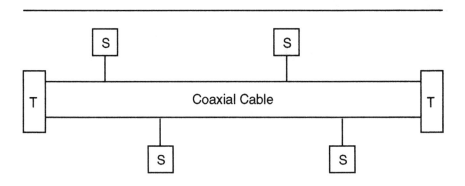

Note: S represents stations and T represents bus terminators.

Figure 4.1. Topology of an Ethernet network.

Notice in Figure 4.1 that all the stations are attached to a common coaxial cable. The bandwidth ranges from 1 to 10 megahertz.

The media is passive and is very reliable. The coaxial cable used is reasonably flexible and can even be bent enough to go around corners. Installation is not complicated because the coaxial cable can be run under floors or above dropped ceilings. Each transmitting station uses the entire bandwidth and transmits when the media is available. Control of the media is arbitrated by using a method based on contention called carrier sense multiple access with collision detection (CSMA/CD), which is described later in this chapter.

In recent years as more Ethernet networks have been set up, the need for a mechanism of connecting two networks while isolating one set of stations from another has arisen. A device that will connect two Ethernet networks to each other, called a bridge, will allow messages from one station on one network going to a station on the other network to pass through but will block messages going from one station to another station on that same network. The topology of an Ethernet network that contains a bridge is illustrated in Figure 4.2.

From the point of view of the individual station, all stations still appear to be connected to one common network. The bridge is programmed to recognize which messages are for which section of the network and to transparently manage the movement of only those messages that need to go from one section of the network through the bridge to the other section of the network.

A bridge can be used to improve the performance of a network by isolating the network traffic that one set of stations generates from the traffic that another set of stations generates. If no isolation is provided, every station on a network sees every message, whether that message is for that station or not.

Connection to an Ethernet Network

Connection to an Ethernet network consists of several parts, which are illustrated in Figure 4.3.

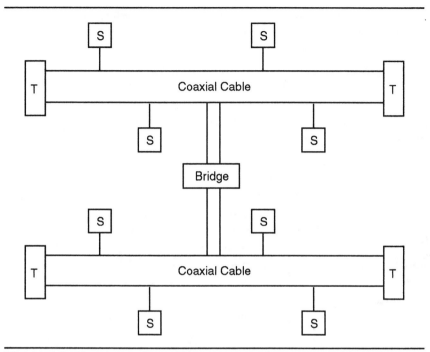

Figure 4.2. Topology of two Ethernet networks connected by a bridge.

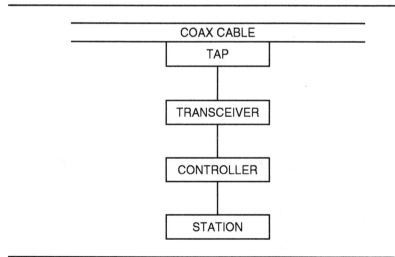

Figure 4.3. Connection to an Ethernet network.

The TAP is a passive physical connection to the cable. Several varieties of taps exist. One type is called a "vampire" tap because a single pin is physically inserted into the coaxial cable. Vampire taps can be used to add a station to a network without disrupting the network. A second type of TAP is the "tee" coaxial cable connector. This type of connection requires no wiring changes but the network will be disrupted when a new station is added.

The TRANSCEIVER listens while it sends (and is thus a combination of transmitter and receiver) and recognizes when messages are interfering with each other (called "collisions"). Some varieties of transceivers are equipped with a series of lights that will blink when the transceiver is receiving or sending, or when collisions are occurring. Such transceivers with lights can be useful, simple network monitoring devices because with them you can get a feeling for the rate of collisions on your network and also whether the device connected to this tap is receiving and transmitting information.

The CONTROLLER knows the address of this port, performs error detection and CSMA/CD management, and breaks the data into packets for transmitting. The controller for the connection can be a board that is inserted into your station. More recent computers, particularly midrange computers, are constructed with an Ethernet controller built onto the cpu board in the computer; to connect to a network requires only a transceiver and a cable.

Finally, the STATION uses this communication system.

A Second Kind of Local Area Network: Broadband Bus

A second kind of local area network can be constructed that does not have some of the limitations that the baseband bus described earlier has. In particular, the total length restriction of only a few kilometers can be hard to adhere to for a company that has a campus of several buildings spread over several city blocks with computers in them that it wants to interconnect.

Characteristics of a Broadband Bus Network

The characteristics of broadband bus networks are:

- Shielded coaxial cable (75 ohm)
- 400 megabits per second bandwidth for cable
- Many separate channels per cable
- 5 megabit per second bandwidth per channel
- Length of network up to ten miles
- Can connect several thousand devices
- Bus arbitration via contention
- No central control in network
- Media is active

A broadband bus network transmits digital data modulated on an analog carrier using frequency modulation or phase modulation. The bandwidth of this medium is up to 400 megahertz. The overall bandwidth is divided into "channels," which have 5 megahertz bandwidth much like cable television systems do for broadcasting different television signals on the same cable. In fact, the broadband medium is used in the very same way that cable television works. The only difference is that the various channels that are used for broadcasting television signals are used for broadcasting digital signals that contain data. Separate channels are created by transmitting a signal modulated on a particular carrier frequency.

Each data channel uses two frequency bands, with one frequency band used for sending and a separate one for receiving. The "headend" of the network retransmits all signals received on the sending channels onto the appropriate receiving channel. This is one difference between broadband buses and baseband buses: broadband buses need extra equipment on the network to service the network itself while baseband buses do not.

The logical view of a data channel in a broadband bus local area network would be as shown in Figure 4.4.

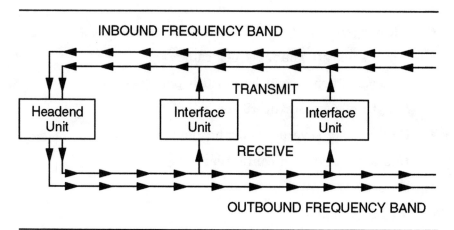

Figure 4.4. Data channel on a broadband bus network.

Using one channel for outbound data and a separate channel for inbound data will achieve full "duplex" operation. The physical network is set up in a tree structure with trunks. Each trunk is connected to the headend for retransmission of the signals. The headend consists of a frequency translator to rebroadcast all inbound streams over all outbound streams, and thus all stations can talk to all other stations that are on the same frequency band.

The medium used for broadband bus systems is also coaxial cable but of a larger diameter than Ethernet cable. To enable the network to cover larger distances, signal amplifiers are used on the medium. Thus the medium is an active part of your network as opposed to baseband systems, which use a passive network.

The topology of such a network is shown in Figure 4.5. Notice that stations in Figure 4.5 are not necessarily on the same piece of coaxial cable.

Control of an individual channel is performed by using contention to determine which station is transmitting data in much the same way that baseband buses work. However, in this case several stations can be transmitting at the same time on different frequencies. Each connection to the broadband bus requires a device that will frequency-shift the transmitting signal to the correct frequency range that matches the channel to which the station is logically connected. In addition, these devices, called interface units, will also have to know which frequency band to receive on. This requires a more complicated connection unit than baseband systems. Much of the hardware for this kind of network is used for cable television systems in large quantities, which has made this type of system much more affordable.

Because the total bandwidth of this medium is divided into separate channels, a particular channel could be used for video transmission instead of data transmission. In addition, telephone equipment is available that can divide a single channel into 64 kilohertz "subchannels," each of which is capable of carrying a telephone conversation. Because the medium carries so many channels, this type of installation is particularly good for universities and colleges, which have many computers scattered over a number of buildings that are physically close to each other but cover a number of miles end to end. In addition, the needs of the various buildings may vary; they include video transmissions and telephone transmissions as well as computer transmissions.

Connection to a Broadband Bus Network

In somewhat more detail, the physical layout of a connection to a broadband bus system would be as in Figure 4.6.

The RF modem selects the appropriate pair of frequencies for receiving and transmitting data and does address recognition and error detection. The network interface controller performs serial-to-parallel conversion of the data.

Taps are physically inserted into the coaxial cable wherever they are needed. The coaxial cable used for broadband bus

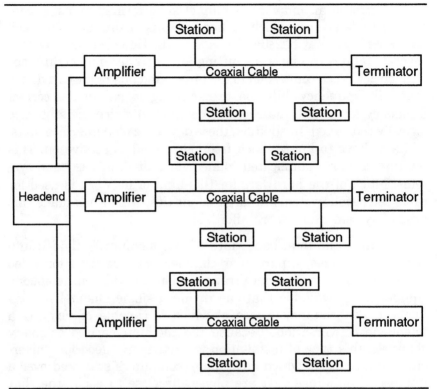

Figure 4.5. Topology of a broadband bus network.

networks is not very flexible and cannot be bent without the use of a special tool made for that operation. It is usually mounted on walls (or ceilings) permanently. Because of this, taps are not easily added to the network. Installing a broadband network is usually done by professional installers.

Controlling Message Transmission on a Bus Network

All stations on a bus network will contend equally for the media but only one station can transmit on the media at a time. Because of this, contention for the media must be controlled.

Three methods exist for controlling transmission on the media: (1) polling, (2) contention, and (3) carrier sense. In a polling-

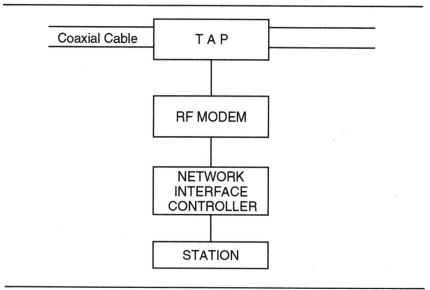

Figure 4.6. Connection to a broadband bus network.

based scheme, the master station requests data from the slave stations, asking each in turn if they have any data to transmit. This is a fairly standard scheme but does not make very good use of the medium. In addition, if the number of stations is very large, the delay in transmitting a message will grow with the number of stations on the network. It would be a lot better if the number of stations had little or no effect on the throughput of the network.

In a contention method, any station can transmit at any time. Transmitting a message is done on one frequency and a second frequency is used to receive on. After the message is transmitted, the station that receives the message will send back an acknowledgment message. If no acknowledgment message is received within a short period of time, it is assumed that the message was not received properly by the destination station; the sending station will wait a random period of time and then send the message again. Since no check of the medium is made before transmitting a message, it is possible for two messages to be sent on the medium at the same time. This is called a "collision" and will result in a message being received that is partially disturbed. The CRC check sums at the end of the message will not be correct and the message will be rejected. A control mechanism like this is used by the University of Hawaii with transmission of signals between stations done by radio frequencies. This kind of contention control will work well in a network characterized by low-volume, bursty traffic.

Another method for controlling the bus is to use the "sense carrier" method. That is to say, if any station is transmitting, no other station can transmit. But when no station is transmitting, any station can transmit. Thus every station is listening all the time even when it is transmitting. This is called a sense carrier method because when a station is transmitting, the signal is imposed on a carrier signal. If a station senses the presence of the carrier on the bus, it is not allowed to transmit. Two stations can still transmit at the same time or at nearly the same time. When this occurs, the two messages will interfere with each other. When collisions occur, both stations will wait a random period of time and then can transmit again if the medium is available. A collision can be detected by all the stations on the network because the message contains CRC error checking.

Combining a contention method and a carrier sense method increases the reliability of the network. Carrier sense multiple access with collision detection (CSMA/CD) requires that each station can listen to the bus and determine if it is busy ("carrier sense"). Once medium is quiet, any station can transmit at once without asking permission ("multiple access"). Each station will listen even while transmitting to make sure that the message is properly transmitted ("collision detection"). If a collision occurs, the transmitting station will send a "jamming burst" to notify all stations of the collision. Then the transmitting station will wait a random time and will try to retransmit the message. An individual station only accepts packets that are addressed to it. Performance is acceptable until the network gets to 30–40 percent loading, and then delays will begin to occur. In this type of network, delivery of messages is not guaranteed. The higher-level protocols that use this type of network implement some type of message sequencing to be able to detect if a message is lost. In addition, messages can be severely delayed on this type of network. Delay of a message will vary with the loading of the network.

Format of a Message on a Bus Network

For local area networks based on bus architectures, a "standard" format of a message has been defined. This definition grew out of a series of papers that were published detailing how this type of network would operate. The format of a message, called a "frame," was then accepted by subsequent software builders. Figure 4.7 shows a schematic view of this message.

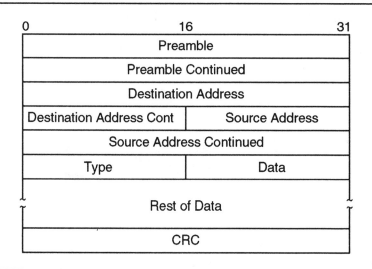

Figure 4.7. Format of a message on an Ethernet network.

The **Preamble** field is a 64-bit pattern of bits for transceivers to use to synchronize on, the **Destination Address** field the address of the destination computer, and the **Source Address** field the address of the source computer. Each address is constructed of six 8-bit fields. The **Type** field is a 16-bit field used to identify the next higher-level protocol for interconnectivity, the

Data field is, of course, user data, and the **CRC** field is a 32-bit field used to do cyclical redundancy-type error checking on the whole message.

Every station on a network must have a unique network address; otherwise, messages will not be reliably delivered. The address of a station is set by the manufacturer of the controller board. Address ranges are assigned to different manufacturers so that unique addresses can be ensured.

Token Ring Local Area Network

Another type of local area network is the Token Ring network. These networks use a ring topology, which is shown in Figure 4.8. In this type of network connections to the cable are made via a ring interface connection. For networks that are large, repeaters may be necessary to amplifier the signal as it moves through the cable.

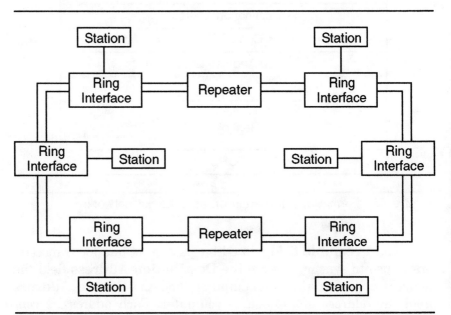

Figure 4.8. Topology of a Token Ring network.

The medium used for Token Rings is twisted pairs of wires or coaxial cable. Both of these are easily installed. The data transmission rate in Token Rings ranges from 100 KHz to 5 MHz. This type of network will need repeaters to perform active signal regeneration because the ring interface units read the data transmitted on the medium and determine if the message is destined for the station attached to it. If the message is not, the message is retransmitted on the media to go to the next station in the ring. In addition, this network is sensitive to cable lengths between repeaters.

Contention is controlled in Token Rings by token passing. In a token-passing scheme the token is transmitted around the bus by repeaters. If a node wants to transmit, it must wait until the token is received and then remove the token from the ring and transmit the packet on the ring. The receiver acknowledges the message and, when the message gets back to the transmitter, the transmitter removes the message and reinserts the token into the network. One advantage of Token Ring networks is that the time that it takes to send a message does not vary, no matter what the message load in the network is.

IBM has implemented the token-passing scheme in a particular manner. In their implementation scheme, a ring consists of a series of nodes connected by a unidirectional transmission path on a closed path. Information on the ring passes from node to node and is regenerated as it passes through each node. Access is controlled by passing a unique bit pattern, the token, from node to node. If a node has no data to transmit, the token is simply passed on. Receipt of a token gives permission to the receiving node to initiate a transmission.

Summary

This chapter has provided a brief introduction into the world of local area networks (LANs). A deeper discussion is beyond the scope of this book. A few of the early papers discussing LANs are: Schoch, J. F., Y. K. Dalal, D. D. Redell, and R. C. Crane,

Computer (August 1982): 10–27; Stallings, W. *Computing Reviews* 16 (1984): 3–41; and Strole, N. C., *IBM J. Res. Develop.* 27 (September 1983): 481–496.

A large number of books discuss various aspects of LANs and should be consulted for more information on this topic.

5

Internet Protocol: Network Layer Protocols

Introduction

The network layer of TCP/IP provides the services necessary to move data from one node to another node even if the nodes are on different physical networks. To accomplish this goal, this layer contains one major protocol to move the data from node to node, the Internet Protocol (IP), and several other protocols (which will be discussed in the next chapter) to solve other node-to-node communications problems.

In order to move data from one node to another efficiently, there are two services that this protocol layer must offer. First, a function must exist that can determine a route through the network to deliver the data to the uniquely identified remote host. Second, functionality must be provided so that messages can be broken up into pieces if an intervening network is unable to handle the large size of the message. Both of these functions will be discussed. In addition, sending messages to a group of hosts via two different methods will be discussed.

Overview of Internet Protocol

Returning once again to a model of the TCP/IP protocols mapped against the functions required by the OSI model of networks, we see that the network layer is the one that enables data to move from one node to another. As Figure 5.1 illustrates, the network layers on cooperating nodes are in communication with each other. Intermediate nodes in this model only need to have the network layer in order to perform their function of moving the data to another node that is logically closer to the destination. Higher and lower layers are only involved as requesters and servers.

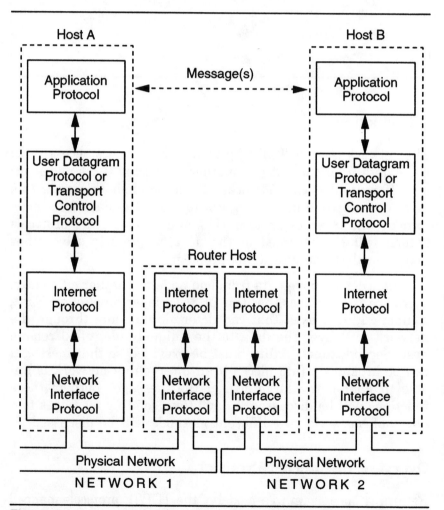

Figure 5.1. Layered model of two communicating hosts.

The two major services that the Internet Protocol layer provides are addressing (to deliver messages from one host to another host) and fragmentation (to move messages through networks that have differing packet sizes).

Figure 5.2 illustrates where the Internet Protocol fits into a layered model of TCP/IP.

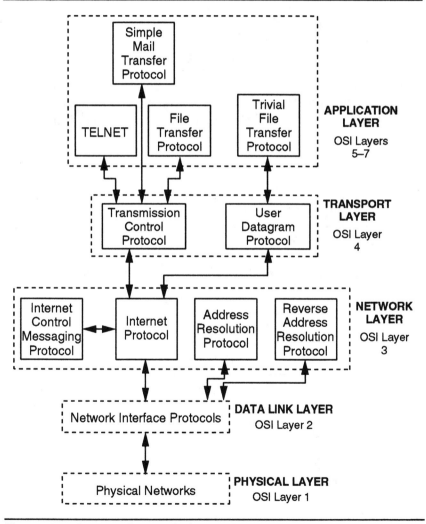

Figure 5.2. Internet Protocol's interaction with other TCP/IP protocols.

Internet Protocol Explained

The Internet Protocol provides an unreliable connectionless method of delivering data from one host to another. It is unreliable because it does not guarantee delivery and provides no sequencing to ensure that the data units are received in order. No acknowledgment is required of any participating hosts. It is connectionless because no "initialization" sequence is necessary for one host to connect with another using the IP layer. The data are packaged in a unit called a packet. Each packet of data is independent of any other packet of data.

As illustrated previously in Figure 3.5 in Chapter 3, the internet layer adds a header to the data that is passed to it from the transport layer before it passes that data to the data link layer. The layout of this header is shown in Figure 5.3.

0 4 8		16 19	31
Version | Lngth | Type of Srvc		Total Length	
Identification		Flags	Fragment Offset
Time to Live | Protocol		Header Checksum	
Source Address			
Destination Address			
Options			
Data			

Figure 5.3. Structure of the Internet Protocol header.

In the Internet Protocol header, the **Version** field identifies format of header used (usually the value "4"). The **Length** field specifies the header-only length in 32-bit words while the length of both the header and the data, measured in octets, is carried in the **Total Length** field. The **Type of Service** field indicates the quality of service desired during the transmission of this message through the internet system. For example, a message can be designated for high or low delay, normal or high throughput, normal or high reliability. Priority messages can be given special treatment by network facilities if so indicated via the Type of Service field. Applications request a particular level of service when they pass their message to this layer. The **Identification** field uniquely identifies this packet so that it can be distinguished from other packets and is usually assigned when data is passed to the network layer from a higher layer. The **Flags** field indicates whether this message is fragmented and whether this is the last message fragment. The **Fragment Offset** field is the offset from the start of the original packet that this fragment is and is used to rebuild the full message once all the fragments have been collected at the destination host (see later discussion). This value is expressed in units of eight octets, or 64 bits. The **Protocol** field specifies the next level of protocol used in the data portion of this internet datagram. Some values for this field are shown in Table 5.1. The **Time to Live** field specifies how long the datagram will be stored on the network before it is destroyed. A time limit must be specified so that if there is an error on the network and some fragment is lost, the other pieces of the original message will be destroyed at some later time and not continue to use the resources of the network. In addition, datagrams can be created for destinations that can cause the datagram to endlessly loop through the internet using the resources of the internet. The current recommended default time is 64. The **Header Checksum** field is used to provide error checking on the header by itself. The **Source Address** and **Destination Address** are the internet addresses of the hosts of interest. The **Options** field is used for specifying routing options, security options, and network testing. One setting of the options field requests that the route this packet takes be recorded in the packet. Another option indicates that the routing through the network is specified in this packet and should be used.

Decimal	Protocol
0	Reserved
1	Internet Control Message
2	Internet Group Management
3	Gateway-to-Gateway
4	IP in IP (encapsulation)
5	Stream
6	Transmission Control
7	UCL
8	Exterior Gateway Protocol
9	Any private interior gateway

Table 5.1.   Some assigned Internet Protocol numbers.

Fragmentation of Packets

Individual routers may have to change the size of the message because it may not be possible for a particular router to handle the largest size message. The identification, offset, length, and flags fields are used together to enable segmentation of packets as they travel through the network from source to destination. The identification is assigned when the packet is initially passed to the network layer to be transmitted to the destination host. At a particular intermediate router, it may be necessary to break up the packet into smaller fragments. This process is called **fragmentation**. The original message divided into shorter size pieces, transmitting each as a different datagram. Each datagram is created with the same header as the first message but it would have an offset that points at where this part of the message would be placed when reconstructing the original packet. If this was the last piece of the original packet, the "more" flag would be off. The offset flag is counted in units of eight octets (or 64 bits). As an example, Table 5.2 shows breaking up a larger datagram into a number of smaller ones.

The identification field is used by the receiving host to gather all the various pieces of the message to be reassembled. The offset is used to place the pieces in the correct order to reconstruct the original message.

Original Datagram:
    Data Length = 850
    Identification = 1
    Offset = 0
    More = 0
First Fragment:
    Data Length = 240
    Identification = 1
    Offset = 0
    More = 1
Second Fragment:
    Data Length = 240
    Identification = 1
    Offset = 30
    More = 1
Third Fragment:
    Data Length = 240
    Identification = 1
    Offset = 60
    More = 1
Last Fragment:
    Data Length = 130
    Identification = 1
    Offset = 90
    More = 0

Table 5.2.   Fragmentation of packet into smaller messages.

Routing Messages from One Node to Another

Routing is accomplished by maintaining routing tables in each station that indicate for each destination network the next router this packet should be sent to. The routing is dynamic and the router needs to be able to "learn" the shortest pathway to a particular network. The Internet Protocol provides several ways for the router to learn about its surrounding networks.

One of the option fields found in the Internet Protocol header requests that each router record in the packet what routers were traversed in moving this packet from source to destination. This kind of information could be used by intermediate routers to understand what pathways through the network are used to reach certain hosts.

Internet Addressing

Each host in a network must have a unique address assigned to it in order for messages to be uniquely sent to a particular host. These addresses (called **internet addresses**) are 32 bits long and are usually displayed in the format X.X.X.X where X is eight bits long and can have any value from 0 to 255. Addresses in this format are often called "dotted decimal" addresses. Each host also has a unique name assigned to it, and that name and the host's internet address can be used interchangeably in sending messages to a particular host if the name and address has been registered in the */etc/hosts* file or if a name server is available. For more information, see Chapter 8, Administering a TCP/IP Network.

Internet addresses are divided into several classes, each of which are illustrated in Figure 5.4. The first five bits in the address are used to indicate which class of address is meant. Class A addresses have "0" as value of the first bit, Class B addresses have "1 0" as the value of the first two bits, Class C addresses have "1 1 0" as the value of the first three bits, Class D addresses have "1 1 1 0" as the value of the first four bits, and Class E addresses have "1 1 1 1 0" as the value of the first five bits. Thus addresses that start with a value between 1 and 126 are class A addresses (addresses that start with 0 or 127 are special addresses and are discussed later). Class B addresses have starting values between 128 and 191, while Class C addresses have starting values between 192 and 223. Class D addresses cover the range from 224 to 239, while Class E addresses cover the range from 240 to 255.

Using dotted decimal addressing, for example, "1.2.255.4" is a class A address, "129.30.3.30" is a class B address and "193.33.33.33" is a class C address. Class A addresses are for networks that have lots of hosts on a single network, while Class C addresses would be for a network with fewer hosts.

Only 126 different Class A networks can exist, with each network having more than 16,000,000 (256*256*256) hosts on it. The values of 0 and 127 are reserved for special purposes. With such a limited number of these kind of networks available, only very large networks use this type of addressing. Most networks do not have that many hosts so this type of addressing is for networks that are organized by subnets (see later discussion).

Up to 16384 (64*256) different Class B networks can be created with 65536 (256*256) hosts on each network. While more than 65000 may seem to be a large number of hosts for a particular network, some company-wide networks will have easily this many hosts where many "terminals" (really diskless workstations) will be networked alongside the servers. Subnets will be useful for this kind of network as well.

More than 2,000,000 (32*256*256) different Class C networks can be created with only 256 hosts on each network. For a small company or other institution this type of addressing would be appropriate. Subnets can be used here, too, to simplify routing tables.

Class D addresses do not identify networks but instead are used to identify special addressing modes. The principal use is for multicasting (see later discussion of multicasting messages). Class E addresses are reserved for future use and have been used for some experimental addresses.

Internet addresses are assigned by a central agency so that an international network (of smaller networks) can be created with each having a unique address. (See Appendix A for more information on the agency that manages this process.)

When setting up a network that does not intend to communicate with networks in the "outside world," an institution can choose any class of network addressing to use. When communicating with a network in the outside world, an institution will have to abide by the addressing standards imposed by that network's administrative group. For the national networks such

0 1 2 3 4	8	16	24	31
0	Network ID <7 bits>	Host ID <24 bits>		

a. Class A Address

0 1 2 3 4	8	16	24	31
1 0	Network ID <14 bits>	Host ID <16 bits>		

b. Class B Address

0 1 2 3 4	8	16	24	31
1 1 0	Network ID <21 bits>		Host ID <8 bits>	

c. Class C Address

0 1 2 3 4	8	16	24	31
1 1 1 0	Multicast Address <28 bits>			

d. Class D Address

0 1 2 3 4	8	16	24	31
1 1 1 1 0	Reserved for Future Use <27 bits>			

e. Class E Address

Figure 5.4. Various classes of internet addresses.

as uunet, bitnet, and so forth, a central agency (the SRI Corporation) assigns network addresses to ensure that the addressing will be unique.

Hosts may have more than one address if they are connected to more than one network. These kinds of multiaddressed hosts, sometimes called multihomed hosts, are usually gateways, or bridges to other networks. They will usually contain more than one network interface board and may support more than one protocol or more than one network medium. In this way, for example, Token Ring networks can be connected to Ethernet networks.

Since an internet address consists of a network ID and a host ID, gateways only need to know the location of other networks, not the location of every other host on that network, in order to correctly route a message to another network.

Subnet Addressing

An organization with an assigned internet address can subdivide the available host address space in any way that it chooses. One possible way is to create **subnets**, or networks within networks. The goal of any network approach is to be able to add hosts with a minimum of disruption to the rest of the network. Forming subnets provides the ability to add hosts easily to a network that contains a number of gateways.

In a networking system gateways need to have knowledge of where every host is located so that when a message needs to be sent to a particular host, the gateway will know a pathway to that host. Adding a new host requires that every routing table in each gateway must be updated. If you are setting up an addressing scheme for Class B internet addresses using subnets, for example, one could use eight bits of the Host Id as the Subnet ID, as shown in Figure 5.5. The gateway can Figure out what route to use to send a message to any particular host without having knowledge of each individual host by just examining the Subnet ID. In this example, a class B type of internet address is used. Using a subnet address of eight bits allows for 254 subnets (the values of 0 and 255 are reserved), each of which can have up to 254 different hosts on it (usually values of 0 and 255 are not used for host addressing).

0 1 2 3 4	8	16	24	31
1 0	Network ID <14 bits>	Subnet ID <8 bits>	Host ID <8 bits>	

Figure 5.5. Class B internet address with an eight-bit subnet ID.

One way to illustrate the principle of using subnet addresses is seen in Figure 5.6, where a network with several hosts is shown. Notice that Host 4 and Host 7 are gateways connecting two separate networks.

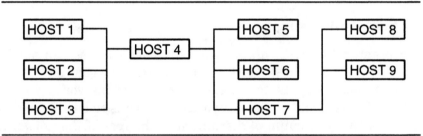

Figure 5.6. Typical network with nine hosts.

How would addresses be assigned to the hosts in this network? A simple way would be to just assign the addresses in numerical order, as shown in Table 5.3.

If we were to create subnets, we could create addresses that would allow the gateways to know where to send a message without examining the entire network table. Table 5.4 illustrates what the network addresses would be if a number of subnets were created.

If Host 1 sends a message to Host 8, the gateways need only examine the subnet part of the address to determine how routing through the network would go. In addition, addition of another host in Subnet 3, for example, would not require changing the routing tables at all.

Name of Host	Internet Address
Host 1	131.3.3.1
Host 2	131.3.3.2
Host 3	131.3.3.3
Host 4	131.3.3.4
	131.3.3.5
Host 5	131.3.3.6
Host 6	131.3.3.7
Host 7	131.3.3.8
	131.3.3.9
Host 8	131.3.3.10
Host 9	131.3.3.11

Table 5.3. First table of hosts and addresses.

Name of Host	Subnet ID	Host ID	Internet Address
Host 1	1	1	131.3.1.1
Host 2	1	2	131.3.1.2
Host 3	1	3	131.3.1.3
Host 4	1	4	131.3.1.4
	2	1	131.3.2.1
Host 5	2	2	131.3.2.2
Host 6	2	3	131.3.2.3
Host 7	2	4	131.3.2.4
	3	1	131.3.3.1
Host 8	3	2	131.3.3.2
Host 9	3	3	131.3.3.3

Table 5.4. Second table of host addresses using subnet addressing.

Every host in a network has to be able to determine the length of the subnet ID field. One type of Internet Protocol (ICMP) has two special message types for this purpose. It is convenient for subnets to use contiguous bits for the subnet number of a network, but this is not a requirement. ICMP address mask request and reply messages enable a network to use noncontiguous bits for a subnet mask and to be able to inform other networks of their use. See the next chapter for more detail on how ICMP messages work.

Broadcasting Messages

Hosts sometimes need to find information about a network or about a host without knowing exactly which host has that information. For example, a diskless workstation may not know its own internet address and may want to request some other host to notify it of its proper internet address. In addition, one host might have information that an entire group of hosts should have. For example, one host might have determined that a particular host is now operating as a gateway to another network, and any message addressed to that network should be sent to this particular host. How can one host inform others of its network knowledge? One method would be to send a message to each and every host with the information of interest. Or if information was needed, the request for information could be in a message that was sent in turn to each host until the information was received. This approach would lead to a flood of messages sent to a range of different hosts in order to gain some information about the network; it would not be an efficient way to send information around a network. Instead a separate class of addressing rules was created with the purpose that any host that fits the addressing criteria can reply to the request for information or receive the information in the message. This messaging methodology is called **broadcasting**.

The following set of addressing rules define which hosts are being addressed when broadcasting messages (these addresses can only be used as destination addresses):

- 255.255.255.255 denotes a broadcast message to *all* hosts on a *local* hardware network; these messages must not be forwarded to any other network through a gateway.

- 36.255.255.255 denotes a broadcast to *all* hosts on the *specific network* #36. If the message is a request for information, any host on network #36 can reply. If this network is using subnet addressing, this message is a broadcast to all subnets on network #36.

- 36.40.255.255 denotes a broadcast to *all* hosts on the *specific subnet* #40 on the *specific network* #36. (Address 36.40.255.255 is a Class A network, thus 40 cannot be part of the network address. As a further example, the address 195.40.255.255 is a broadcast to all hosts on the network 195.40 because this is a Class C address.)

- 127.0.0.1 denotes a broadcast to the *local host* only and acts as a local loopback address. Any messages sent to this address must not be sent out on the network but instead must be echoed back to the host.

The following set of rules define special addresses that can be used as source addresses in a broadcast message:

- 0.0.0.0 denotes *this* host on *this* network. This special address is used by a workstation that does not know its internet address in a message that requests information about its own internet address. (See the ICMP discussion in the next chapter.)

- 0.0.0.27 denotes a *specified* host on *this* network. This special address can be used by hosts that do not know the network number (or subnet number) that they are part of.

For networks that are using subnet addressing, a broadcast to all hosts on a subnet would be to put in all 1s as the host address. If the subnet addressing is as in the network in Table 5.4, a broadcast to Subnet 3 would use a destination address of 131.3.3.255.

Multicasting Messages

A multicast message is one that is transmitted to a group of hosts on a network. The constitution of a group of hosts is dynamic, and hosts may join and leave a group at any time. Multicast messages can even be sent to groups of hosts that are not on the local network. Host group addresses are those with 1110 as the high-order four bits (what was earlier called "Class D addresses"). In dotted decimal notation these group addresses range from 224.0.0.0 to 239.255.255.255. Two addresses in this range are special: 224.0.0.0 is guaranteed not to be assigned to any group, and 224.0.0.1 is assigned to the permanent group of all IP hosts that will both receive and send multicast messages (usually gateways). Some of the currently assigned group addresses are listed in Table 5.5. Other permanent groups will be assigned by the Internet Architecture Board as needed. Sending a multicast message is simply to code in the address of one of the destination groups as the destination address and otherwise treat the message in a standard way.

To handle group-oriented messages, the Internet Group Management Protocol (IGMP) was developed. This protocol is considered part of the IP layer of the TCP/IP Protocol suite. Two of the new operations added permit hosts to join a host group or to delete themselves from a host group. In addition, a Host Membership Query message may be used to determine if a particular host is a member of a particular group, and a Host Membership Report message is sent when the membership of a group changes.

Summary

In this chapter the functionality of the Internet Protocol has been examined with emphasis on the message fragmentation and addressing functions that the Internet Protocol performs. An example of message fragmentation is used to illustrate how messages are fragmented when moving through networks that have smaller message sizes. The layout of the internet header is discussed with emphasis on the way particular fields in the header are used. The various classes of internet addresses are illustrated, and subnet addressing is shown to simplify routing

Multicast Address	Assigned to:
224.0.0.0	Reserved
224.0.0.1	All Systems on this Subnet
224.0.0.2	All Routers on this Subnet
224.0.0.3	Unassigned
224.0.0.4	DVMRP Routers
224.0.0.5	OSPFIGP All Routers
224.0.0.6	OSPFIGP Designated Routers
224.0.0.7	ST Routers
224.0.0.8	ST Hosts
224.0.0.9	RIP2 Routers
224.0.0.10-224.0.0.255	Unassigned
224.0.1.0	VMTP Managers Group
224.0.1.1	NTP (Network Time Protocol)
224.0.1.2	SGI-Dogfight]
224.0.1.3	Rwhod
224.0.1.6	NSS – Name Service Server
224.0.1.9	MTP Multicast Transport Protocol
224.0.1.10-224.0.1.255	Unassigned
224.0.2.1	"rwho" Group (BSD) (unofficial)
224.1.0.0-224.1.255.255	ST Multicast Groups
224.2.0.0-224.2.255.255	Multimedia Conference Calls

Table 5.5.   Assigned internet multicast group addresses.

tables. Addresses used for broadcasting and multicasting messages are examined to determine how to create an address that addresses only those hosts of interest.

The complete discussion of the Internet Protocol is found in RFC 791. Several additional RFCs cover various addressing issues including subnets (RFC 917), broadcasting (RFC 922), and multicasting (RFC 1112). For lists of the assigned values for the Protocol field, the Version field, the multicast addresses, and the Type-of-Service values, RFC 1340, "Assigned Numbers," would be examined.

6

Other Internet Protocols: ARP, RARP, and ICMP

Introduction

As discussed in a previous chapter, the Internet Protocol is used to move data from node to node. Problems that can interfere with this data movement are managed by a group of associated protocols that interact with the Internet Protocol (see Figure 6.1).

Address Resolution Protocol (ARP) offers the network interface protocols in the data link layer the capability of translating software addresses to hardware addresses; Reverse Address Resolution Protocol (RARP) provides the ability to translate hardware addresses into software addresses. Internet Control Message Protocol (ICMP) provides many of the error-reporting mechanisms that can be used to regulate the performance of the network.

Address Resolution Protocol (ARP)

The internet address of a node is a software-assigned set of numbers, but the "real" address that the data link layer software knows nodes by is a hardware address. For example, every Ethernet transceiver has an address that is unique, and that address will need to be used by the data link layer of other nodes to send message to that node. For other hardware-based networks, different addressing schemes exist to solve the same problem: addressing messages to the desired host using its hardware address. The network layer of TCP/IP uses the internet address as its method to address a particular node. But how does the data link layer translate an internet address into a hardware address, such as the Ethernet address?

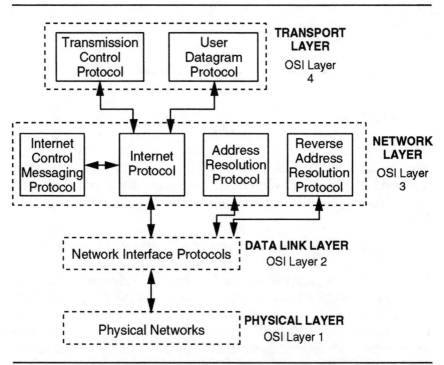

Figure 6.1. Internet Protocol interaction with other TCP/IP protocols.

Giving each node an internet address that is used by the Internet Protocol only enables the Internet Protocol layer to be isolated from the hardware and data link layers that use their own methods of addressing nodes in a network. Thus the Internet Protocol is not dependent on any particular hardware addressing scheme. Unfortunately, this independence is not without its cost: some service must be available that will provide the hardware address of a node in a network if its internet address is known. To solve this problem for the Internet Protocol, the Address Resolution Protocol (ARP) was developed.

ARP is a protocol that maps internet addresses to hardware addresses. Even though the ARP function is provided as a required part of the IP layer, the data link layer uses the ARP function directly.

Nodes that will be communicated with are often registered in a file that contains their internet address but not their hardware address. See, for example, the discussion of the /etc/hosts file in Chapter 8, "Administering Your TCP/IP Network." Yet the data link layer will need the hardware address to send messages to the correct node. The ARP server can be requested by the data link layer to inform it what the hardware address of the internet host is. The composition of the data packet that ARP uses to determine the translation is shown in Figure 6.2.

0	8	16	31
Type of Hardware		Type of Protocol	
HdwrLngth	SftwrLngth	Message Opcode	
Hardware Address of Sender (N Bytes)			~
Protocol Address of Sender (M Bytes)			~
Hardware Address of Target (N Bytes)			~
Protocol Address of Target (M Bytes)			~

Figure 6.2. ARP data packet.

In order to provide the ability of ARP to support different hardware platforms (and thus isolate Internet Protocol from the hardware and data link layers), the ARP data packet contains flags to indicate what kind of hardware and which protocol is being serviced and what length each of their addresses are. ARP can manage translation of any of the various hardware addresses because the length of the hardware address is specified in the request and reply packet itself. The **HdwrLngth** field indicates the length of each hardware address (shown in Figure 6.2 as N bytes long), and the **SftwrLngth** field indicates the length of each protocol address (shown in Figure 6.2 as M bytes long). For example, Ethernet hardware addresses are 48 bits in length while other hardware addresses are somewhat shorter. Table 6.1 lists some hardware types and protocols that are supported by ARP.

For ARP to operate as an address translator, only two function codes are needed: (1) ARP REQUEST code, which asks for address translation and (2) ARP REPLY code, which indicates that this packet contains the reply to an ARP request. Both the hardware and software addresses of the target host and the sender host are contained in the packet.

For ARP requests a packet will be sent out that contains the internet address of the sender (and the hardware address of the sender) and the internet address of the target with no hardware address filled in. The opcode is set to ARP REQUEST. Such a packet using Ethernet as the hardware layer is illustrated in Figure 6.3.

This packet will be broadcast to the network. When such an address resolution packet is received by the target node, the receiving Ethernet module will forward that packet to the ARP process on that node to reply to. Other nodes may record the address of the sending node but they will not reply to the message, even if they have the information requested. Thus ARP operates in the same layer as the Internet Protocol, as an adjunct to it. The ARP process that receives this packet will move the sender addresses into the target addresses and will fill in the hardware and Internet Protocol addresses of the sender with its own hardware/protocol addresses, as shown in Figure 6.4. The opcode of the ARP packet is changed to ARP REPLY and the message is sent back to the originating node.

Hardware Type	Description
1	Ethernet (10Mb)
2	Experimental Ethernet (3Mb)
3	Amateur Radio AX.25
4	Proteon ProNET Token Ring
5	Chaos
6	IEEE 802 Networks
7	ARCNET
8	Hyperchannel
9	Lanstar
10	Autonet Short Address
11	LocalTalk
12	LocalNet (IBM PCNet or SYTEK LocalNET)
13	Ultra Link
14	SMDS
15	Frame Relay
16	Asynchronous Transmission Mode (ATM)

Protocol Type		Description
Dec	Hex	
512	0200	XEROX PUP
513	0201	PUP Addr Trans
1536	0600	XEROX NS IDP
2048	0800	DOD IP
2049	0801	X.75 Internet
2050	0802	NBS Internet
2051	0803	ECMA Internet
2052	0804	Chaosnet
2053	0805	X.25 Level 3
2054	0806	ARP
2055	0807	XNS Compatibility
2184	0888	Xyplex
2304	0900	Ungermann-Bass net debugr
2560	0A00	Xerox IEEE802.3 PUP
4096	1000	Berkeley Trailer nego
4097	1001	Berkeley Trailer encap/IP
5632	1600	Valid Systems
16962	4242	PCS Basic Block Protocol
21000	5208	BBN Simnet
24576	6000	DEC Unassigned (Exp.)
24579	6003	DEC DECNET Phase IV Route

(and many more)

Table 6.1. ARP-supported hardware and protocol types.

0	8	16	31
0	1	8	0
6	4	0	1
11	11	11	11
11	11	192	11
11	11	0	0
0	0	0	0
193	36	20	20

Figure 6.3. Sample ARP request packet for an Ethernet LAN.

0	8	16	31
0	1	8	0
6	4	0	2
11	11	11	11
11	11	192	11
11	11	44	33
22	11	22	33
193	36	20	20

Figure 6.4. Sample ARP REPLY packet for an Ethernet LAN.

In addition, the ARP process will add the hardware address, protocol address, and protocol type to a table that the ARP process maintains. If this set of information is already in the table, that entry is updated. This action will allow ARP to resolve the next address request if it is necessary to do so in the future. For large complicated networks with many nodes, preloading this translation table might be more efficient than having ARP REQUEST and REPLY messages being generated and floating around the network. A command can be used to inform ARP of known software address and hardware address couplets. This command takes the form

arp -s   InternetAddr   HardwareAddr

where "InternetAddr" is the internet address and "HardwareAddr" is the hardware address for that host. Using a set of these commands when starting up a network will eliminate ARP message traffic.

With the length of the hardware address and the length of the protocol address included in the ARP packets, support of different types of hardware addresses is possible. In addition, the ARP module need not know what hardware method is used because it gets its hardware addresses from the messages it receives from other ARP modules.

Since ARP requests are broadcast to all nodes on a network, it is not an error if a particular node does not reply. All ARP requests received are used to maintain a translation table that contains protocol type, protocol address, hardware type, and hardware address for nodes in the network. If the target protocol address or hardware address matches the protocol address of a particular node, that node must reply to the ARP request packet. If the node whose internet address is in the message fails to reply, it is assumed that the node is no longer in service. The ARP translation table can be displayed by entering the command

arp -a

and the display will look like

```
host1.localcomp.com (198.129.31.3)  at  2:60:8c:42:29:93 [ethernet]
host2.localcomp.com (198.129.31.4)  at  2:60:8c:2f:d3:2b [ethernet]
host3.localcomp.com (198.129.31.5)  at  0:80:2d:0:2f:e9 [ethernet]
host4.localcomp.com (198.129.31.6)  at  aa:0:4:0:1:4 [ethernet]
host5.localcomp.com (198.129.31.7)  at  2:60:8c:a4:69:30 [ethernet]
```

indicating for a remote host what its internet address and hardware type and address is.

Reverse Address Resolution Protocol (RARP)

How can a node in a network determine its own internet address if all it knows is its hardware address? To solve this problem, Reverse Address Resolution Protocol (RARP) protocol was developed.

Reverse Address Resolution Protocol (RARP) is a protocol that will map hardware addresses to internet addresses. In particular, diskless workstations need to know the hardware address of the node that will be booting it up. In addition, the data link layer will need to translate hardware addresses into internet addresses so that it can determine which host sent a particular message. This translation is provided by using the Reverse Address Resolution Protocol.

Some diskless workstations that are loaded by other workstations in a network may not know their own internet address. In order for the loading of their software to succeed (usually using tftp services), the internet address of the workstation will need to be determined. The RARP server can be requested to provide this address. The basic packet that RARP uses is the same one that ARP uses as previously illustrated in Figure 6.2. One additional opcode (3) is used to inform the target of the message that RARP address translation is needed. A second additional opcode (4) is needed to inform the sender of the initial RARP message that this message contains the response to the RARP request.

A diskless workstation usually knows its own hardware address and the hardware address of the device that will load its software, usually called the "boot" device. But it won't know the internet address of its boot device and usually won't know its own internet address. RARP provides the ability for the diskless workstation to send out a packet with just the information that it knows and get back a reply that contains the missing information.

The node desiring to determine its own internet address would broadcast a packet that is like the one in Figure 6.5. In this example, a node that has a hardware address of 11.22.33.44.55.66 is requesting that the node whose hardware address is 44.44.44.44.44.44 provide its internet address. Ethernet addresses and internet addresses are used as examples. The reply packet as illustrated in Figure 6.6 indicates that its internet address is 196.6.7.8 and the internet address of the node that was requested for information is 193.3.4.5.

Internet Control Message Protocol (ICMP)

The Internet Control Message Protocol (ICMP) is handled by the TCP/IP protocol itself and not user processes. It is used by TCP/IP to report errors and transfer control information between gateways and hosts. ICMP uses IP as a higher-level protocol even though it is an integral part of IP. ICMP encapsulates IP packets just like the data layer will. Figure 6.7 details the contents of ICMP messages. The **Type** field indicates which kind of message this is. The **Code** field denotes a particular kind of error for an error response and has other values for other message types. The **Checksum** field is used to ensure that the entire ICMP message has not been corrupted. For a number of messages, **Identifier** and **Sequence Number** fields are used to match "request" messages with "reply" messages.

0	8	16	31
0	1	8	0
6	4	0	3
11	22	33	44
55	66	0	0
0	0	44	44
44	44	44	44
0	0	0	0

Figure 6.5. Sample RARP REQUEST REVERSE packet for an Ethernet LAN.

0	8	16	31
0	1	8	0
6	4	0	4
44	44	44	44
44	44	193	3
4	5	11	22
33	44	55	66
196	6	7	8

Figure 6.6. Sample RARP REPLY REVERSE packet for an Ethernet LAN.

0	8	16	31
Type	Code	Checksum	
Different uses for different message types			
Internet Protocol Header including Originating Address and Destination Address ~ ~			
64 Bits of Original Data Packet			

Figure 6.7. Internet Control Message Protocol (ICMP) packet.

Table 6.2 summarizes the different messages that ICMP uses.

Type	Message Use
0	Echo Reply
3	Destination Unreachable
4	Source Quench
5	Redirect
8	Echo
11	Time Exceeded
12	Parameter Problem
13	Timestamp
14	Timestamp Reply
15	Information Request
16	Information Reply
17	Address Mask Request
18	Address Mask Reply
A1	Address Format Request
A2	Address Format Reply

Table 6.2.   Internet Control Message Protocol packet types.

Echo message is sent by a gateway or a host to another gateway or host, and the **Echo Reply** message is returned by the destination host or gateway to indicate that the gateway or host is still operating.

Destination Unreachable message is sent by a gateway to the source address of an IP data packet if that message cannot be delivered to the intended node. A code in the message is set to indicate which component in the network is unreachable and whether the problem is due to unavailability of the node or an incorrect route to the node.

Source Quench message is sent by the host or gateway when it is receiving messages at too rapid a rate or if its buffers are becoming filled and it will be forced to discard messages.

Nodes that receive these messages are supposed to cut back the rate at which they are sending data packets or the receiving node will be forced to discard packets.

Redirect message is sent by a gateway when that gateway determines that the host that sent the message and another gateway that is on the same network as the source host is closer to the destination host than this gateway is

Time Exceeded message is sent when a packet must be discarded because it could not be delivered in the time required.

Parameter Problem message is sent by a gateway or host when it discovers a problem with one of the header parameters that will cause the message to be discarded and not delivered.

Timestamp message is sent by a host to another host, and **Timestamp Reply** message is returned by that host so that the time it takes for a message to get from one host to another can be determined.

Information Request and **Information Reply** messages are sent by a host to determine its own network number.

Address Mask Request message is sent by a host or a gateway to determine what subnet mask is being used on a subnet on a network. The host or gateway that knows the subnet mask will send the subnet mask to the requesting host or gateway in an **Address Mask Reply** message. (It is not enough to know the number of bits in the subnet mask because it is entirely possible that the subnet mask is not a contiguous set of bits.)

Address Format Request message is sent by a host or a gateway to learn the number of bits in the subnet part of the internet address for a particular network. The **Address Format Reply** message contains the number of bits in the subnet part of the address in the *code* field in the ICMP message.

Summary

This chapter has focused on the various protocols in the internet layer other than the Internet Protocol itself, which was discussed in the previous chapter. Each of these protocols assists the Internet Protocol to move data from one node to another. Address Resolution Protocol translates internet addresses into hardware addresses that the network interface protocols can use. Reverse Address Resolution Protocol translates network interface protocols into internet addresses. In addition, reporting of errors in the network is provided by the Internet Control Message Protocol.

Address Resolution Protocol is described in RFC 826, Reverse Address Resolution Protocol in RFC 903, and Internet Control Message Protocol in RFC 792. The various "ASSIGNED NUMBERS" for TCP/IP are listed in RFC 1340 and forms the basis for Table 6.1. Some subnet addressing issues are discussed in RFC 917 and RFC 950.

7

User Datagram and Transmission Control Protocols: Transport Layer Protocols

Introduction

In the layered view of TCP/IP, the User Datagram Protocol (UDP) and Transmission Control Protocol (TCP) provide the service that application programs need: raw data delivery. As previously shown in Table 3.1 in Chapter 3, UDP and TCP provide different kinds of services. Applications can choose which protocol provides the kind of services that they need. Figure 7.1 illustrates which protocol is used for several applications and displays how UDP and TCP fit into this model of TCP/IP. Both UDP and TCP use the Internet Protocol as the underlying protocol.

This chapter is concerned with examining UDP and TCP and their functionality and structure in order to understand how each of these protocols provides the various services that it does.

User Datagram Protocol (UDP)

The User Datagram Protocol (UDP) provides a method for one application to send a message to another application on another network without requiring that the destination application be active when the message is sent to the destination network. UDP is a datagram-based protocol that does not guarantee delivery, and does not guarantee protection against duplicate datagrams. The one advantage of UDP is that it requires a minimum of services to move data from one host to another. The structure of the UDP packet is shown in Figure 7.2.

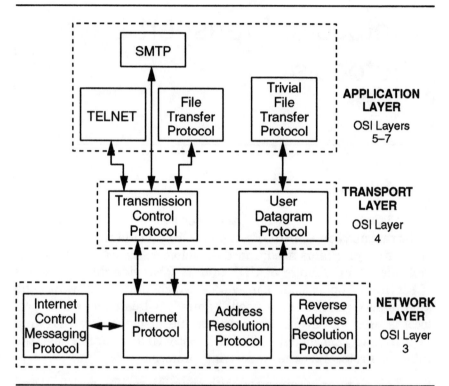

Figure 7.1. How UDP and TCP interact with other TCP/IP protocols.

0	16	31
Source Port	Destination Port	
Length	Checksum	

Figure 7.2. Structure of the User Datagram Protocol header.

In the UDP header, the **Source Port** is used to provide identification of the source of this message. This field does not need to be filled in because there is no requirement for the host that receives this data to reply to the source of the data. If this field is not valid, it must be filled with zero. The **Destination Port** field is used to provide identification of the destination port. The port for a particular application can be determined by examining a table of "well-known" ports such as those shown later in Table 7.1. The overall **Length** of the packet (in octets) includes the length of the UDP header as well as the length of the data portion of the datagram. The **Checksum** field checks the entire datagram including the header and the data.

This is a connectionless message delivery, and UDP considers the message delivery complete once the message is placed on the network. The messages are queued until the receiving applications are ready for them. While the check sum calculation can be used to ensure that the message is correctly received, the messages are not numbered and thus are unsequenced. This type of message delivery is not reliable but can be used for such activities as trivial file transfer to start up a diskless workstation.

The UDP process must be able to determine the source and destination internet addresses and the protocol field from the internet header, which follows the UDP header. Usually the entire datagram including the Internet Protocol header and the UDP header are delivered to the application that is using UDP services.

Transmission Control Protocol (TCP)

Transmission Control Protocol (TCP) provides a highly reliable stream of packets between transport layers on internet hosts by requiring an acknowledgment from the receiving transport layer within a specified period of time and by providing a sequence number to ensure that the packets are delivered in the order that they were sent. Error checking of each packet is provided by a check sum transmitted as part of the TCP header. TCP makes no assumption as to the reliability of the lower-level protocols. To achieve this level of control and reliability, connection from the transport layer on one host to another must be set up before data can be transferred. Figure 7.3 illustrates the information that the transport layer adds when using TCP protocol. TCP's services are used by applications that desire reliable data transmission between hosts. TCP provides a means to recover from lost or damaged data and provides a means to control the rate at which data is transmitted.

0	4	10		16		31
Source Port					Destination Port	
Sequence Number						
Acknowledgment Number						
Data Offset	Unused	U R G	A C K	P S H	R S T	S Y N	F I N	Window
Checksum						Urgent Pointer	
Options							Padding

Figure 7.3. Structure of the Transmission Control Protocol header.

In the TCP header, the **Source Port** field identifies the port number of a source application program, while the **Destination Port** field identifies the port number of the destination application. Thus many data streams can be set up between the same two hosts using different port numbers. The **Checksum** field is 16 bits long and is used to verify both the integrity of the segment header and the data. The **Data Offset** field specifies the offset from the beginning of the message that the data occupies in the message in 32-bit words.

The **Sequence Number** field specifies the sequence number of this segment of the message and is used to ensure that the segments of a message can be ordered properly and can be acknowledged individually. The **Acknowledgment Number** field contains the sequence number of the next segment expected to be received and indicates correct reception of all messages up to that sequence number. Thus each message can contain both a new message sent to the remote host and the acknowledgment of a received message. As each acknowledgment is received, the segment of the message that it acknowledged is discarded from a "retransmission" queue. If a segment of a message is not acknowledged within a set period of time, that segment is retransmitted.

A set of bits in the middle of the header is used for controlling the connection between the two applications. Each bit has a different function: the **URG** bit for noting that the Urgent pointer is valid, the **ACK** bit for noting that the Acknowledgment field is valid, the **PSH** bit to cause the data in the message to be "pushed" through to the receiving application even if the buffer is not full, the **RST** bit for resetting the connection, the **SYN** bit for resynchronizing the sequence numbers, and the **FIN** bit for marking that the sender has reached the end of its byte stream.

Flow control is handled via the **Window** field, which specifies how much data the receiver is willing to accept before another acknowledgment must be received by the sender. The window value is specified when the connection between the applications is established. If one application cannot accept more data from the other, the window field would be set to zero.

At the end of the header is room for the variable-length **options** field, which is used to indicate the maximum segment size.

Establishing and Closing Connections

A connection between the application on one host and the application of the other host must be established before data can be exchanged between them. A connection is established by the exchanging of several messages, as illustrated in Figure 7.4. TCP on Host A initiates the connection by sending a SYN message with an initial sequence number to TCP on Host B (message #1). TCP on Host B acknowledges reception of SYN message from A and transmits its own SYN message with its own initial sequence number (message #2). TCP on A acknowledges the SYN message of B (message #3) and the connection is established. This is called a three-way (or three-message) handshaking. Initial sequence numbers are chosen based on a fictitious clock that cycles every 4.55 hours. A time-based mechanism is used to avoid reusing sequence numbers too frequently. If a SYN request is received by a TCP process that is not in the ESTABLISHED stage, a reset message must be sent and the connection is closed so that a new connection can be reopened properly synchronized.

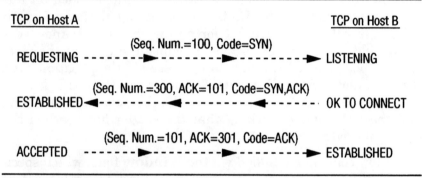

Figure 7.4. Establishing a TCP connection between two hosts.

A connection is closed by sending a message with the FIN bit set on, indicating no more data to send. No more messages will be sent after that but messages can still be received and acknowledged in the normal way. After the FIN message has been acknowledged and a FIN message has been received from the other side of the connection, the connect can finally be closed. Figure 7.5 illustrates this sequence of message exchanges.

The connection is finally closed after FIN messages have been acknowledged by both sides of the connection.

Addressing a Particular Application on a Remote Host

As discussed in an earlier chapter, every node must have a unique network address called an internet address. On that

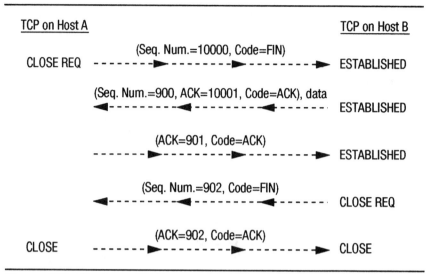

Figure 7.5. Closing a TCP connection between two hosts.

node, several applications using TCP/IP services can be executing at the same time. How can messages that are destined for one particular application on a particular node be separated from messages destined for another application? The internet layer only passes messages from one node to another node and packages the messages without regard to their application destination. A second level of addressing is used for addressing the particular application of interest; this type of addressing is called port number addressing.

When an application starts to use TCP/IP services, it can request an application-based address, a port number. Port numbers are 16 bits long and are assigned by the transport layer. If an application needs to use a particular TCP/IP service, it can do so by addressing that service using a "well-known" port number, which is preassigned. A list of some of these port numbers is given later in Table 7.1. These port numbers are registered in a file called /etc/services (discussed in detail in Chapter 8). The well-known services such as ftp, telnet, etc., register their port numbers in this file. For example, ftp uses port number 21 for its service requests, while tftp uses port number 69. When a user executes a TCP/IP command such as ftp, the application will send a message to the well-known port number on the node of interest. The port number of the requesting application will be in the initial message so that the application on the remote host knows the full address of the requesting application. Port numbers are protocol-dependent, and the UDP and TCP protocols used in the transport layer can use the same duplicate port numbers because the protocol being used is also in the initial message. Typically both the same UDP and TCP port numbers are assigned to the well-known services even though the service may only use one or the other.

Unique port numbers must be used by the applications because another application using that same port number will get messages that are destined for another application. Port numbers used by one application can be registered in the /etc/services file so that another application does not use it. Once the port number has been registered, other applications that wish to communicate with a particular application can look in the /etc/services file to find out what port number to use. For some services the port number of the requesting application is checked to be sure that it is one of the restricted ones and not one being used by a user application.

A unique connection between two applications can be described by five pieces of information:

Protocol Being Used

Internet Address of Local Node

Port Number of Application on Local Node

Internet Address of Remote Node

Port Number of Application on Remote Node

Thus the full description of an association between two applications would be five pieces of information and can be shown as

(TCP, 142.17.3.2, 2145, 142.17.3.3, 21)

which might be the description of a connection to FTP on the host with the address 142.17.3.3.

Port numbers less than 1024 are reserved for specific services. User applications use port numbers that are larger than 1024 but less than 64000. In Table 7.1 some of the port numbers of the well-known services are listed. For example, when

Service Name	Port Number		Description of Service
	0/tcp &	0/udp	Reserved
tcpmux	1/tcp &	1/udp	TCP Port Service Multiplexer
rje	5/tcp &	5/udp	Remote Job Entry
echo	7/tcp &	7/udp	Echo
discard	9/tcp &	9/udp	Discard
systat	11/tcp &	11/udp	Active Users
daytime	13/tcp &	13/udp	Daytime
qotd	17/tcp &	17/udp	Quote of the Day
chargen	19/tcp &	19/udp	Character Generator
ftp-data	20/tcp &	20/udp	File Transfer [Default Data]
ftp	21/tcp &	21/udp	File Transfer [Control]
telnet	23/tcp &	23/udp	Telnet
smtp	25/tcp &	25/udp	Simple Mail Transfer
dsp	33/tcp &	33/udp	Display Support Protocol
time	37/tcp &	37/udp	Time
nameserver	42/tcp &	42/udp	Host Name Server
nicname	43/tcp &	43/udp	Who Is
login	49/tcp &	49/udp	Login Host Protocol
domain	53/tcp &	53/udp	Domain Name Server
bootps	67/tcp &	67/udp	Bootstrap Protocol Server
bootpc	68/tcp &	68/udp	Bootstrap Protocol Client
tftp	69/tcp &	69/udp	Trivial File Transfer
finger	79/tcp &	79/udp	Finger
hostname	101/tcp &	101/udp	NIC Host Name Server
nntp	119/tcp &	119/udp	Network News Transfer Protocol
ntp	123/tcp &	123/udp	Network Time Protocol
exec	512/tcp		Remote process execution; authentication performed using passwords and UNIX login names
biff	512/udp		Used by mail system to notify users of new mail received
who	513/udp		Maintains databases showing who is logged in to machines on a local net and the load average of the machine
cmd	514/tcp		Like exec, but automatic authentication is performed as for login server
printer	515/tcp &	515/udp	Spooler
timed	525/tcp &	525/udp	Timeserver
uucp	540/tcp &	540/udp	uucp daemon

Table 7.1. Some well-known port numbers.

a client contacts the ftp server on a particular host, it uses the well-known port number of the ftp server (21) and asks the TCP server for a local port number to include in the message so that the ftp server can send back responses to the requester of ftp services.

Comparison of Services TCP and UDP Provide

The transport layer of TCP/IP has two different possible choices: UDP and TCP. An application chooses one of these two protocols to use. Since they offer different services, an application chooses based on which level of service it needs. Table 7.2 compares the services that these two protocols provide. While TCP offers many more services than UDP does, implementation of an application using TCP will be more complicated. Thus UDP is suiTable for simpler applications like Trivial File Transfer Protocol and booting diskless workstations.

Service	UDP	TCP
Connection oriented?	N	Y
Message Boundaries?	Y	N
Data Checksum?	Optional	Y
Positive Acknowledgment?	N	Y
Timeout and Retransmit?	N	Y
Duplicate Detection?	N	Y
Sequencing?	N	Y
Flow Control?	N	Y

Table 7.2. Comparison of services UDP and TCP provide.

Summary

This chapter has examined the two protocols that TCP/IP offers in this layer: User Datagram Protocol (UDP) and Transmission Control Protocol (TCP). UDP provides an unreliable, unconnected, datagram-based service, while TCP provides a reliable, flow-controlled, connection-based, segment-based service. Both of these services address a particular application on a host using a port number that allows one data stream between the same two hosts to contain messages for several application-to-application communication streams.

UDP is described in great detail in RFC 791, while TCP is similarly described in RFC 793. The Table of TCP/IP Port Assignments is from the RFC entitled "Assigned Numbers" (latest version is RFC 1340) written by J. Reynolds and J. Postel and is available from the RFC source as discussed in Appendix A.

8

Administering a TCP/IP Network

Introduction

Earlier chapters have described how the various protocols in the TCP/IP Protocol suite cooperate to move data from one application on one host to a second application on a second host. Other chapters have described how various TCP/IP applications provide various functions for users in a networked environment. Some parts of this software need information to operate effectively; this information is organized in a series of files.

Part of the administration of a TCP/IP network is to manage the contents of a number of files that control the TCP/IP network functions. Each of the files performs a specific purpose and needs to be maintained if all of the various functions of a TCP/IP-based network are to work properly.

The hosts File

Nodes in a network are registered in a file called */etc/hosts*. Any node named in this file can be sent messages if its name is known. Nodes that are not in this file can still be sent messages but only if their internet address is known or a name server is running. A typical */etc/hosts* file is shown in Figure 8.1. Each entry in the file shows first the internet address and second at least one name for that node on the network. Multiple names can be specified for any computer on the network. The first name listed is usually thought of as the name of the node; the other names are called *alias names*. Any alias names for the host can be included by being entered on the same line as the internet address for that node. This file is used to translate the name of a host into an internet address.

127.0.0.1	localhost		
192.129.16.11	host1	host1alias	host1anothername
192.129.16.12	host2	host2alias	
192.129.16.13	host3	host3alias	

Figure 8.1. Contents of a typical */etc/hosts* file.

Examining the typical */etc/hosts* file shown in Figure 8.1, the host name host1 has the internet address of 192.129.16.11 and two alias names of host1alias and host1anothername. The internet address and name of the local host must be in this file because the local host will use the contents of the */etc/hosts* file to determine its own internet address. The address 127.0.0.1 is a special address reserved for testing the local network software.

The "Equivalent Hosts" File

The *hosts.equiv* file in the */etc* directory lists the names of hosts that are permitted to execute certain remote commands such as **rsh**, **rcp**, and so forth, on the local host without supplying a password. (For a description of what each of these commands do, see the appropriate chapter in this book.) This file is often called the "equivalent hosts" file because each of the hosts in this file can perform many of the same commands that the local host can perform. In addition, the same user name must be defined on the remote host as the user name on the local host although the passwords can be different. Some implementations do not allow the user name to be "root." The **rlogind** server, **rshd** server, and

lpd server check the *\/etc\/hosts.equiv* file before executing the requested command. Each entry in the *\/etc\/hosts.equiv* file as illustrated in Figure 8.2 consists of the name of the host that is permitted to execute commands on the local host. This host name must also be in the *\/etc\/hosts* file.

---

host1

host2

host3

host4

host5

Figure 8.2. Contents of a typical *\/etc\/hosts.equiv* file.

As many names of hosts can be listed as desired. They are listed one name to a line.

The rhosts File

The *.rhosts* file specifies the names of remote users who are not required to supply a login password when they execute the **rcp**, **rlogin**, and **rsh** commands using a local user's account when the remote user and the local user are not the same. This file is placed in the local user's **home directory** as specified in the *\/etc\/passwd* file. This file must be owned by the local user and its permissions must restrict access to the local user only. The existence of this file allows access to one's files from remote hosts and thus this file should be created and populated carefully. If the ownership and the permissions on the file are not set correctly, most implementations of TCP/IP servers will ignore this file and refuse access to a remote user.

A sample *.rhosts* file as shown in Figure 8.3 contains entries that list the name of the remote host and the name of the user on that remote host that is requesting access to the local user's files. Each pair of names, remote host and remote user, must be on separate lines and must be separated by blanks or tabs.

host4	sam
host5	jerry
host6	fred
host6	samantha

Figure 8.3. Contents of a typical *.rhosts* file.

If the sample *.rhosts* file was in the home directory of sally and was owned by Sally and had permissions of "600" (read/write only by owner), the user named *sam* from the host *host4* or the user named *jerry* from the host *host5* could login to Sally's account without specifying a password.

The netrc File

The *.netrc* file provides information used by the **ftp** and **rexec** commands to automatically connect to a host without a password. This file is placed in a user's home directory (as specified by the environment variable $HOME or as specified in the */etc/passwd* file) and must be owned by the user and have access permissions that permit reading by owner only.

A sample *.netrc* file is shown in Figure 8.4 and contains the keyword "machine" and the name of the host, the keyword "login" and the name of the user, and the keyword "password" and password of the user separated by spaces, tabs, or new lines. The keywords must be included as shown but entries can be on several lines.

machine	host4	login	sam	password	goodtimes
machine	host5	login	jerry	password	jerrypass

Figure 8.4. Contents of a typical *.netrc* file.

When the **ftp** command or the **rexec** command executes, the *.netrc* file in the home directory of the user on the local host is read to be able to supply the user name and password from the remote host. Thus the example in Figure 8.4 specifies that when the remote user logs into *host4* as a user named *sam*, the password to specify is *goodtimes*.

The Password File

The *passwd* file in the /*etc* directory contains the names and passwords of all the users that are authorized to access this particular host. Most network commands will fail if the user in whose name the command is executed is not defined on the remote host. The password that a user has on different hosts need not be the same. The password can be specified in the /*etc*/*passwd* file but might not be, for security reasons.

In addition, the /*etc*/*passwd* file contains several other important pieces of information. The various fields that each entry in the /*etc*/*passwd* file contains is shown in Figure 8.5. Each field is separated from the others by a colon (":"). A typical entry in the /*etc*/*passwd* file is shown in Figure 8.6.

Field	Meaning of field
User Name	Login name of user
Password	Encrypted password for this user or exclamation point ("!") if stored somewhere else
User ID	Numeric string, usually uniquely identifying the user to be used in attaching ownership to files
Group ID	ID of group that user belongs to
User Information	Miscellaneous string, usually identifying user; often user's full name
Home Directory	Full path name of directory that contains user's files
Shell Name	Name of shell program to start when user logs in

Figure 8.5. Fields in the /etc/passwd file.

---

martya:!:234:78:Marty Arick:/jerico/home/martya:/bin/csh

Figure 8.6. Sample entry in the */etc/passwd* file.

The Home Directory listed in the */etc/passwd* file for a particular user is the directory that the user will be placed in when logging in from a remote host.

The services File

The */etc/services* file specifies for a particular application the port number and protocol that application uses. This file is used by the various servers to determine what port to listen at for requests for the particular service that the server provides. Figure 8.7 illustrates a typical */etc/services* file. For user-written applications that will use TCP/IP services and need to use a port to listen at or to send messages from, it is a good idea to add entries to the */etc/services* file so that other servers can make sure that they do not use ports already being used by other applications. Port numbers less than 1024 are reserved for system applications.

An operating system call can be used to find the port number for a particular application on the local host. Port numbers for various TCP/IP services are assigned by a central agency (Internet Application Board) so that any other service that wishes to communicate with one of those TCP/IP services on a remote host will know what port number to use. As stated previously, these ports are called "well-known" port numbers. Services can be added and port numbers assigned to them but these port numbers must not use any of the well-known and previously assigned port numbers.

Each entry in the */etc/services* file consists of the official internet service name, the port number used for that service, which transport layer protocol is used, and any unofficial names (aliases) that service might be known as. For example, in the example file, the ftp server uses port 21 for communications and uses TCP as its Transport Protocol.

echo	7/udp		
discard	9/udp	sink null	
systat	11/tcp		
daytime	13/tcp		
netstat	15/tcp		
ftp	21/tcp		
telnet	23/tcp		
mtp	25/tcp	mail	
time	37/tcp	timeserver	
name	42/tcp	nameserver	
whois	43/tcp		
mtp	57/tcp		# deprecated
nicname	101/tcp	hostname	# usually from sri-nic

```
#
# Host specific functions
#
```

tftp	69/udp		
rje	77/tcp		
finger	79/tcp		
link	87/tcp	ttylink	
supdup	95/tcp		
pop	109/tcp		# Post Office Protocol

```
#
# UNIX specific services
#
```

uucp	251/tcp		# MASSCOMP specific
exec	512/tcp		
login	513/tcp		
shell	514/tcp	cmd	# no passwords used
courier	530/tcp	rcp	# experimental
biff	512/udp	comsat	
who	513/udp	whod	
syslog	514/udp		
talk	517/udp		
route	520/udp	router routed	# 521 also
timed	525/udp	timeserver	

Figure 8.7. Contents of a typical */etc/services* file.

Testing Network Connections

As part of the network layer providing message routing from one host to another, TCP/IP provides one protocol (the Internet Protocol) to move packets from one host to another and a second, called Internet Control Message Protocol (ICMP), to support the determination of the physical path through the network from one host to another. One of the services that ICMP performs is "echo responding," which means that when a node receives a ECHO_RESPONSE message from another host, it is required to send an acknowledgment back to that host. Thus if it were desired to determine whether a node was connected to a network and responding, another node could send an ICMP message to that node and expect a response. If no response was received in a reasonable period of time, it would be assumed that node was not on the network.

The command that sends the ECHO_RESPONSE message to another host is called the **ping** command. (Some have claimed that the name of this command is short for "Packet InterNet Groper.") This command is usually found in the /etc directory with other system-oriented commands. The simplest form of this command,

   ping   host1

sends messages to the host *host1* and measures how long it takes for the reply to be received. This process is repeated as long as desired. If no response is received, the command will hang and not return. Each receipt of a message is usually accompanied by output that indicates how long the round trip to the remote node is. Receiving responses from a remote node is proof that the remote node is connected and properly defined on the local host. Usually the **ping** command will indicate what internet address it is using for that remote host. It is possible to use an internet address in place of the name of the host if the particular host of interest is not yet defined on the local system.

The **ping** command has several options that can be used to examine the performance of your network. By default, the packet size that **ping** uses is 64 bytes. A different packet size can be specified on the command line, as in

ping   host1   1024

which would send packets of 1024 bytes to the remote host named *host1*. The time that this size packet takes to make the round trip to the remote host is a measure of how the network is performing. It is also possible to specify how many times to send the message to the remote host, as in

ping   host1   1024   25

which would send packets of 1024 bytes to the remote host named *host1* 25 times and then stop and print a summary of the timings.

Finally, it is possible to use the **ping** command to determine pathways through a network by specifying the "-o" option on the command. Thus the command

ping   -o   host1

would list the intermediate internet hosts that were traversed in getting the message from the local host to the remote host.

Examining Network Performance

The performance of the network can be analyzed by using a variety of techniques, the most basic of which is the **netstat** command. The **netstat** provides several different sets of output depending on which option is chosen. The **netstat** command will display different types of information about the various parts of the network setup.

For example, the performance of the network interface hardware can be examined by using the **-v** option on the **netstat** command. Figure 8.8 shows the output from **netstat -v**.

The memory that is allocated to the network routines can be examined by using the **netstat -m** command, as illustrated in Figure 8.9.

ETHERNET STATISTICS (en0):
Hardware Address: 02:60:8c:2e:09:04

Transmit Byte Count: 18134446	Receive Byte Count: 6520501
Transmit Frame Count: 43757	Receive Frame Count: 57285
Transmit Error Count: 0	Receive Error Count: 0
Max Netid's in use: 7	Max Transmits Queued: 1
Max Receives Queued: 0	Max Stat Blks Queued: 0
Interrupts Lost: 0	WDT Interrupts Lost: 0
Timeout Ints Lost: 0	Status Lost: 0
Receive Packets Lost: 0	No Mbuf Errors: 0
No Mbuf Extension Errors: 0	Receive Int Count: 57285
Transmit Int Count: 43757	CRC Error Count: 0
Align Error Count: 0	Recv Overrun Count: 0
Packets Too Short: 0	Packets Too Long: 0
No Resources Count: 0	Recv Pkts Discarded: 1172
Xmit Max Collisions: 0	Xmit Carrier Lost: 0
Xmit Underrun Count: 0	Xmit CTS Lost Count: 0
Xmit Timeouts: 0	Parity Errors: 0
Diag Overflow Count: 0	Execute Q Overflows: 0
Execute Cmd Errors: 0	Host Side End of List Bit: 0
Adpt Side End of List Bit: 0	Adapter Pkts to Be Uploaded: 57285
Adapter Pkts Uploaded: 57285	Start Receptions to Adpt: 1
Receive DMA Timeouts(lock up): 0	

Figure 8.8. Output from **netstat -v** command for Ethernet.

158/384 mbufs in use:
     1 mbufs allocated to data
     4 mbufs allocated to packet headers
     59 mbufs allocated to socket structures
     84 mbufs allocated to protocol control blocks
     2 mbufs allocated to routing table entries
     6 mbufs allocated to socket names and addresses
     2 mbufs allocated to interface addresses
0/46 mapped pages in use
232 Kbytes allocated to network (8% in use)
0 requests for memory denied

Figure 8.9. Output from **netstat -m** command.

The state of the current connections between hosts can be displayed by using the **netstat -n** command, as shown in Figure 8.10. In this display the port number of the application on each host is attached to the internet address of that host with the type of protocol being used shown to the left of each entry. ESTAB indicates that the connection is established.

Active Internet connections

Proto col	Recv Queue	Send Queue	Local Address	Foreign Address	(state)
tcp	0	0	130.151.158.148.513	130.151.156.103.1020	ESTAB
tcp	0	0	130.151.158.148.1026	130.151.156.59.6000	ESTAB
tcp	0	0	130.151.158.148.1025	130.151.156.59.6000	ESTAB

Figure 8.10. Output from **netstat -n** command.

The current state of the routing tables is displayed by the **netstat -r** command, while statistics about the various protocols are shown with the **netstat -s** command. The statistics for the *tcp* protocol are shown in Figure 8.11, and the statistics for the *icmp* protocol are shown in Figure 8.12.

The command **netstat -i** will show the state of the various hardware interfaces, and **netstat -id** will show the state of the interfaces with the count of dropped packets, as illustrated in Figure 8.13.

Summary

This chapter has concentrated on reviewing the contents and purpose of the various files that are used by the TCP/IP software. The *hosts* file identifies the various hosts in the network, while the equivalent hosts file (*hosts.equiv*) identifies remote hosts whose users can perform the same commands on the local host as the local users. The *.rhosts* file specifies remote users who are permitted to operate in the home directory of a local tcp:

    14307 packets sent

        13251 data packets (9654670 bytes)

        0 data packets (0 bytes) retransmitted

        992 ack-only packets (927 delayed)

        0 URG only packets

        6 window probe packets

        9 window update packets

        49 control packets

    13894 packets received

        4535 acks (for 2927337 bytes)

        24 duplicate acks

        0 acks for unsent data

        3089 packets (94703 bytes) received in-sequence

        0 completely duplicate packets (0 bytes)

        0 packets with some dup. data (0 bytes duped)

        28 out-of-order packets (798 bytes)

        0 packets (0 bytes) of data after window

        0 window probes

        194 window update packets

        0 packets received after close

        0 discarded for bad checksums

        0 discarded for bad header offset fields

        0 discarded because packet too short

    18 connection requests

    17 connection accepts

    35 connections established (including accepts)

    38 connections closed (including 2 drops)

    1 embryonic connection dropped

    9795 segments updated rtt (of 1 attempts)

    1 retransmit timeout

        0 connections dropped by rexmit timeout

    0 persist timeouts

    0 keepalive timeouts

        0 keepalive probes sent

        0 connections dropped by keepalive

Figure 8.11. Output from **netstat -s** for tcp protocol.

icmp:

        17 calls to icmp_error

        0 errors not generated 'cuz old message was icmp

        Output histogram:

                destination unreachable: 12

        0 messages with bad code fields

        0 messages < minimum length

        0 bad checksums

        0 messages with bad length

        Input histogram:

                echo reply: 3

                destination unreachable: 32

                source quench: 2

                routing redirect: 2

                time exceeded: 3

        0 message responses generated

Figure 8.12. Output from **netstat -s** for icmp protocol.

Name	Mtu	Network	Address	Ipkts	Ierrs	Opkts	Oerrs	Coll	Drp
lo0	1536	<Link>		342	0	342	0	0	0
lo0	1536	127	localhost	342	0	342	0	0	0
en0	1500	<Link>		679020	0	581046	0	0	0
en0	1500	168.238.11	test.host.com	679020	0	581046	0	0	0
et0	1492	<Link>		23391	0	10131	0	0	0
et0	1492	none	none	23391	0	10131	0	0	0

Figure 8.13. Output from **netstat -id** command.

user without specifying the local user's password. The *.netrc* file specifies users and remote hosts that can connect to the local host without specifying a password. The *password* contains the information that describes a user of the local system.

The *services* file specifies the port number that a particular remote TCP/IP service uses.

For further information, you can examine the manual pages that describe that files that have been discussed in this chapter. The manual pages for the **ping** command and the **netstat** command review many other options for the commands that were not discussed in this chapter.

9

Overview of TCP/IP
Applications

Introduction

The previous chapters have concentrated on the protocols of TCP/IP and how they work together. The next chapters will focus on the standard applications that have been created to solve certain networking problems that users have. Table 9.1 summarizes the applications that are available, showing the command that invokes the particular application and the chapter in which it is discussed. This chapter outlines what the particular applications do.

Operation	Command	Chapter
Logging into a Remote System	rlogin	10
Connecting to a Remote System	telnet	11
Copying Files from Host to Host	rcp	12
Executing Commands on Remote Host	rsh	13
Simple File Transfer	tftp	14
Transferring Files Between Hosts	ftp	15
Electronic Mail Services	mail	16
Accessing Remote Files Locally	mount	17
Miscellaneous Network Services		18

Table 9.1. TCP/IP standard applications.

Logging into a Remote System (rlogin Command)

Users desiring to run commands interactively on a remote host can use the **rlogin** command to establish a connection on the remote host and cause the login command to be started in the name of the requesting user. Unless otherwise specified, the requesting user is the user who executed the **rlogin** command on the local host. Once the connection is established, all further keystrokes entered on the local host are passed to the remote host, and all output generated on the remote host is displayed on the terminal of the local host. An optional argument can be used to invoke a login session on a remote host in the name of a different user.

Connecting to a Remote System (telnet Command)

Users desiring to connect to a remote system and interact with any of the various servers on a remote system can use the **telnet** command. Executing the **telnet** command with just the name of the remote host will cause a login session to begin on the remote host. **telnet** commands are available to control the connection with the remote host. The **telnet** command models all terminals as "Network Virtual Terminals," which are simplified ASCII devices with keyboards and printers. Support of more advanced terminal functions is negotiated between telnet client and server. Telnet support is available on a wide range of disparate computer systems.

Copying Files from Host to Host (rcp command)

Copying files from one host to another is most easily accomplished using the **rcp** command. Whole directories can also be copied with one command. Ordinarily the command operates in the name of the user on the local system that invoked it, but optional arguments can be used to specify the names of other users under which to perform the command. Files remote from the local host can be copied from one remote host to another.

Executing Commands on a Remote System (rsh Command)

Commands can be executed on a remote host without logging into it by using the **rsh** command. The output from the command is returned to the local host as if the command was executed on the local host. Any host to which the user has access can have commands executed on it. Normally the commands are executed on the remote host in the name of the user on the local host that executed the **rsh** command, but an optional argument can be used to identify a different user under which the command on the remote host will be executed.

Simple File Transfer (tftp Command)

Transferring one file from one system to another can be accomplished using the **tftp** command. Only reading or writing files is supported and no validation of the command is performed. No directory operations are performed. **tftp** uses UDP as its transport protocol, thus implementation of **tftp** is simplified. **tftp** is suitable for loading diskless workstations.

Transferring File Between Hosts (ftp Command)

Transferring groups of files between hosts is accomplished using the **ftp** command. Moving between both the local and remote directories and listing contents of directories are supported functions. Multiple selection criteria can be used to select which files to transfer. A command language is available to create scripts of file transfer commands.

Electronic Mail Services (mail Command)

Properly formatted messages can be sent from one user to another user without the sender knowing where the receiving host is. These messages are usually called "mail messages" and can be sent anywhere in a network by invoking the **mail** command. A complete mail address contains two elements, the first of which is the name of the user on the remote host, and the second being the network address of the remote host. The Mail Protocol depends on the other protocols to route the message properly to the destination user.

Accessing Remote Files Locally (mount command)

Files that are physically located on a remote host can be made locally accessible using Network File Services. Executing a **mount** command can enable a remote file system to appear to a user to be a local file system. Users can treat these network file systems as local file systems.

Miscellaneous Network Services

A variety of optional network services are available to use as network test tools or to use to set a standard date and time throughout a network. One service will echo back to the requesting host any characters it is sent, while another will send back to the requesting host all of the printable ASCII characters. Two different time services are available: one will return the current date and time, while another will return the number of seconds since midnight, January 1, 1900.

Summary

Applications that use TCP/IP protocol have been summarized in this chapter. The next chapters will discuss each application in detail.

10

Logging into a Remote System (rlogin Command)

Introduction

The **rlogin** command is used to log into a remote host and start an interactive terminal session. Once this session is established, all commands that are executed will be executed on the remote host until the session is ended.

This chapter will examine how to use the **rlogin** command, how the server that supports the **rlogin** command operates, and what problems can occur when executing **rlogin** commands.

How to Use the rlogin Command

The syntax for the **rlogin** command is

rlogin   RemoteHost

which will log the local user onto the specified remote host *RemoteHost* and connect the local terminal that the command was entered on to the remote host. The remote terminal type will be the same as the local environment variable TERM. The window size will be the same as the one on the local host if the remote host supports that particular window size. Ctrl-S and Ctrl-Q key sequences are used to stop and start the flow of information. Input and output buffers will be flushed on interrupts.

The **rlogin** command will run the "login" command on the remote host to start a terminal session under the name of the local user.

If a user wants to login to a remote host under a different name, the "-l" option is available to specify the name of the user under which you want to execute on the remote host. For example,

rlogin   RemoteHost -l UserName

will start an interactive terminal session on the remote host *RemoteHost* under the name "UserName." The interactive session will be started in the Home directory (see description of the *etc/passwd* file in Chapter 8), and the environment will be what the user "UserName" has set up.

If an 8-bit path between the local host and the remote host is necessary, the optional parameter "-8" can be specified. Thus, the command

rlogin   RemoteHost -l UserName -8

will log the user *UserName* onto *RemoteHost* and send and receive 8-bit characters.

The user can interrupt the current login session on the remote host by entering the escape character. By default this escape character is the tilde (~). The escape character will only be recognized as an interrupt if it is the first character on the line, that is, the first character following a carriage return. Entering two escape characters in a row as the first two characters in a line will cause one escape character to be sent to the remote system as an ordinary character. Entering the escape character and a period (.) will cause the connection between the local host and the remote host to be immediately broken.

A different escape character can be specified by using the "-e" option. For example,

rlogin   RemoteHost   -e\

will change the escape character to be a backslash (\) during the login session that is started with this command.

The **rsh** command when run without further parameters will invoke the **rlogin** command and log in the user on the remote host. You can set up linked files and then just enter the name of the remote host that you want to log into. For example, if you link a file as in

ln   -s   /usr/ucb/rsh   RemoteHost

and you execute the command

RemoteHost

a login on *RemoteHost* will be started for the user. The system administrator of the system can create a series of these linked files so that in order to log onto a particular host, the user only needs to type in the name of that host. (A fuller description of how the **rsh** command operates can be found in Chapter 13.) The interactive terminal session on the remote host will continue until the user logs out of the remote host.

Some Examples of Use of the rlogin Command

The simplest example of the use of the **rlogin** command is to enter the command

rlogin   host1

which will start a login session on the remote host *host1* using the same user name as the user that issued the command.

If a user wishes to start a session on a remote host under the user name *sam*, that user would enter the command

rlogin   host1   -l sam

which would start a session on the remote host *host1* under the user name *sam*.

If a user wishes to start a session on a remote host under a user name different from the current user name and use the character \ as the escape character, that user would enter the command

rlogin   host1   -l sam   -e

which would start a session on the remote host *host1* under the user name *sam* with the escape character defined as \.

If a user wishes to start a session on a remote host under a different user name and use 8-bit characters between hosts, that user would enter the command

rlogin   host1   -8   -l   fred

which would start a session on the remote host *host1* under the user name *fred* using 8-bit characters.

Starting a session on a remote host can be as simple as entering the name of the remote host of interest, as in the command

host1

if the system administrator has properly defined commands that execute the **rsh host1** command when only the name of the host is entered.

How the rlogin Server Functions

If the request for connection is received by the rlogin server, the validation process is as follows:

1. The source port number is checked to make sure it is between 512 and 1023 and is thus a trusted requester.

2. The rlogin server validates the client user by looking up the local user's name in the */etc/passwd* file and then changing to the directory listed there. If either the name lookup or the directory change fails, the user is not validated.

If the user id is not 0 (that is to say, it is not the root user), the */etc/hosts.equiv* file is searched for the name of the local host trying to log in. If the name is in the file, the user is validated. If the name of the local host is not present in the file, the Home directory of the user is checked for a *.rhosts* file and that file is searched for the name of the local host.

If the user validation fails, the rlogin server will prompt the user for his/her password, which will be checked in the */etc/passwd* file on the remote host.

After the user is validated, the rlogin server allocates a pseudoterminal (called a "pty") and connects standard input, standard output, and standard error to it.

The rlogin server propagates the baud rate and terminal type as found in the environment variable TERM. The first message that the server receives from the client contains the baud rate and the terminal type.

The window size is requested by the client and the server will attempt to provide that service. This process is called negotiation. Furthermore, if there are changes to the window size during the life of the connection, this too would be requested from the server. The window size is requested by the client by sending a 12-byte message to the server that is detailed in Figure 10.1. By describing the window that is desired, the **rlogin** command is requesting that the **rlogin** server on the remote host provide a similar window.

Byte	1:	Hexadecimal FF
Byte	2:	Hexadecimal FF
Byte	3:	Ascii lowercase "s"
Byte	4:	Ascii lowercase "s"
Bytes	5 and 6:	Number of Character Rows
Bytes	7 and 8:	Number of Characters per Row
Bytes	9 and 10:	Number of Pixels in the x direction
Bytes	11 and 12:	Number of Pixels in the y direction

Figure 10.1. Window size request by **rlogin** client.

As a note: The **rlogin** command is preferred to the **telnet** command because system administrators can set up user validation so that no password is needed for a user to login on another host. The **telnet** command always requires a password to be entered. Unfortunately, this approach, while convenient for users, opens a security hole on the remote system when you use this approach.

What Problems Can Occur With the rlogin Command

The major problem that occurs with the **rlogin** command is that the user on the local system is not known on the remote system. Typically, for this problem the message "No such user" will be received. The solution to this problem is either starting the session on the remote host under another name (using the **-l** option) or having the system administrator of the other system add your name to a list of valid users.

Another problem is that for some types of hosts the **rlogin** command may not be supported. For these hosts, the user should try the **telnet** command because that command is more widely implemented.

Summary

A session can be started on a remote host in order to execute commands on the remote host by executing the **rlogin** command. Once the session is established, all commands entered are executed on the remote host until the session is ended by use of the **logout** command. An optional argument can be used to change the user of the session on the remote host.

For further study look at the manual pages for the **rlogin** command on your particular UNIX host. For more details on the under-the-cover operation of the rlogin command, read RFC 1282, "BSD Rlogin," written by B. Kantor in 1991.

11

Connecting to Remote Hosts (telnet) Command

Introduction

The **telnet** command provides remote login services so that an interactive user on a client system can connect with a server on a remote system. By default the server is the telnet server to provide an interactive terminal session to execute commands on the remote host. But other servers such as the mail server or the ftp server can also be directly connected to. Once a connection is established, the client process on the local host passes the user's keystrokes to whichever server process it was connected with. If that server process was the telnet server, a login session will be started. The telnet command uses TCP as the protocol to ensure error checking.

When the telnet command establishes a connection with a remote host, it maps the local terminal into a model of a terminal called a "Network Virtual Terminal" (NVT), which is described fully later in this chapter. The NVT is an imaginary device that has a printer and a keyboard and can print the full set of 7-bit ASCII characters. Each end of the connection performs the same mapping functions so that neither end of the connection knows (or cares) what kind of terminal is actually being used. Negotiation of the availability of some services will take place with either end of the connection offering a service or requesting a service that needs to be performed by the other end of the connection. This offer can be refused by either end of the connection.

This chapter will examine how to use the **telnet** command, how the server that supports the **telnet** command operates, and what problems can occur when executing **telnet** commands.

How to Use the telnet Command

Entering the **telnet** command in its simplest form,

telnet

will start the telnet process, and the prompt

telnet>

will appear on your terminal. You are now in command mode and can connect to any host. You can also set up the various modes of the **telnet** command, as discussed in a later part of this chapter.

To start a login session with a host, enter the telnet command in the form

telnet   Host

which will establish an interactive login session with the remote host. Specifying the name of the remote host on the command line causes a connection to be made to the remote host. The remote system will prompt for the login name and password. After the connection is made, the command is in input mode and all input is sent to the remote host to be processed there. Input can be character-at-a-time or line-at-a-time. While the connection is maintained, the local mode can be switched from input to command mode.

In command mode the type of input can be switched from character-at-a-time to line-at-a-time or vice versa, and the local echo can be disabled or enabled.

The **telnet** command will attempt to negotiate with the remote host what local terminal type is to be on the remote host. Terminal negotiation is not supported by all telnet hosts. Telnet will attempt to emulate a VT100 terminal. Telnet will also emulate a 3270 terminal if either end of the telnet connection is an IBM computer. Terminal negotiation can be disabled on the requesting hosts. Usually there is an environment variable that will control what characters constitute the alternate telnet escape character other than the default ctrl-T.

The **telnet** command can be used to connect from a Unix system to a remote system that is running VMS because both ends of the connection can emulate a VT100 type of terminal. When a login connection is requested on a remote host, the **telnet** command will negotiate with the *telnet* server on the remote host which terminal type to emulate. This emulation functionality shields from the user any differences in the underlying operating system or hardware that might affect character representations or character ordering in messages. These services would be found in the OSI model in Layer 6, the presentation layer. The **telnet** command can provide these terminal services to the user.

While in the command mode, the command

mode   line

will set the input mode to line-by-line while

mode   character

will set the input mode to be character at a time.

While in the command mode,

open   Host   [Port]

will open a connection to the specific host at the specific port if specified. If no port is given, the telnet server will be connected to the telnet server on the remote host, which will start a login session on that remote host.

To control whether input should be echoed to the local terminal, the variable "echo" can be set on or off to set the local echo on or off. To close a connection with a remote host, enter the command **close**. To get a list of commands, enter the character **?**. To end a telnet session, enter the command **quit**. To get a snapshot of the current status of the connection with a remote host, enter the command **status**. To get a list of the settings of the various modes of the telnet command, enter the command **display**. All of these commands must be issued in command mode, not in input mode. You can switch from input mode to command mode by entering the command **ctrl-T**, that is to say, you press both the ctrl key and the T key at the same time. (This pair of keys can be changed. See instructions later.) You can control how telnet responds to a variety of local and remote events by toggling one of the following parameters.

You would toggle **crmod** to map carriage returns sent by the remote hosts to both a carriage return and a line feed. Use this when the host you are dealing with does not send a line feed with its carriage returns.

You can also control what special characters are used to send control sequences to the remote host for operations such as synchronizing output, interrupting the process on the remote host, and so forth. These special characters are translated by the **telnet** command into special commands that the telnet client process send to the telnet server on the remote host to request services such as erasing characters, flushing output, and so forth. These special services can be requested directly through the **telnet** command mode by entering "send xxxxxx" and the correct argument to the service needed. Multiple arguments can be included on the same request separated by blanks. Table 11.1 lists the argument that you add to the send command that you can use to effect the various services that are needed. Some services have "special character" sequences associated with them; they are listed in Table 11.2.

As an example, to interrupt the process on the remote system, you would go into command mode and enter the command "send ip". You could also enter the local terminal's interrupt character. Such a request can be made at any time but is usually sent because no response from the remote host has been received recently.

Service Required	Send Argument
Abort Output	ao
Break or Kill	brk
Erase Character	ec
Erase Line	el
Send Escape Code	escape
Interrupt Process	ip
Are You There	ayt
Go Ahead	ga
No Operation	nop
Secure Attention Key	sak
Synchronize	synch

Table 11.1. telnet **send** command arguments.

Service Required	Special Char	Default Special Character
Abort Output	flushoutput	Ctrl - O
Break or Kill	quit	Local Terminal Quit Character
Erase Character	erase	Local Terminal Erase Character
Erase Line	kill	Local Terminal Erase Character
Send Escape Code	escape	Ctrl - T
Interrupt Process	interrupt	Local Terminal Interrupt Char

Table 11.2. telnet special character commands.

Several entries in Tables 11.1 and 11.2 require explanation. The send argument "ayt" sends a request to the telnet server asking the telnet server to respond. Such a request can be made at any time but is usually sent because no response from the remote system has been received recently.

The send argument "ga" tells the telnet server to return control to the local user because all the output has been sent to the remote terminal and you should perform the line turnaround function, in that the line is now available to be turned around for transmission from the other end. This is especially valuable for half-duplex lines.

The send argument "synch" causes the remote server to discard all previously typed input that has not been read and processed without dropping the connection. The send argument "sak" causes the remote server to invoke a "trusted shell" if it supports that mode. Normally when telnet connects to another system, the login command is started with the requesting user as a nonprivileged user. If you need privileges, you can request them this way. If the remote system does not support this, the message "Remote side does not support SAK" will be returned.

The operation of these special characters can be controlled by the setting of a variable "localchars". When it is set "off," the special characters (such as "ctrl," etc.) are sent through to the remote host as literal characters. When "localchars" is set "on," these special character sequences are recognized as requesting services of the telnet server.

Some Examples of Use of the telnet Command

The simplest use of the **telnet** command is to establish an interactive terminal session with a remote host to execute commands on that remote host. To do this, enter the following:

telnet   hostname

which will cause the **telnet** command to establish a connection with the remote host named *hostname*; the following will display on your terminal:

    trying ...
    Connection to hostname
    Escape character is "^T"

followed by several blank lines. Then the **telnet** command will start a login session with the host named *hostname*. This remote host will prompt for your login name and then your login password. After both responses have been entered and validated, commands are executed on that remote host from then on until the **logout** command is entered or the telnet session is halted. Entering whatever the "Escape character" was specified as when you connected to the remote host will return control to the local host. These escape sequences will differ depending on what kind of host you are connected to. Once you enter the escape sequence, control will be transferred to the local host (while the connection to the remote host is maintained), and the following will be displayed on the local terminal:

    telnet>

Once connected to a remote host, you can change from character-at-a-time to line-at-a-time or change whether you are sending carriage return/line feed or just line feed by issuing the telnet command. You can also change the special characters that invoke the telnet commands as listed previously in Table 11.2.

Several levels of help and status displays are available. To get a display of information about which commands are available and what they do, enter the following:

    telnet> **help**

the output of which is illustrated in Figure 11.1; then the telnet prompt will again be displayed.

Commands may be abbreviated. Commands are:

close	Close current connection
display	Display operating parameters
emulate	Emulate aVT100 or 3270 terminal
mode	Try to enter line-by-line or character-at-a-time
open	Connect to a site
quit	Exit telnet
send	Transmit special characters ('send ?' for more)
set	Set operating parameters ('set ?' for more)
status	Print status information
toggle	Toggle operating parameters ('toggle ?' for more)
z	Suspend telnet
?	Print help information

Figure 11.1. Available telnet commands.

To find out what the current settings of the various special characters are, enter the following:

telnet> **set ?**

which will display how the various special characters are set up as shown in Figure 11.2.

If you wanted to display how the various toggled options are currently set, you would enter the following command:

telnet> **toggle ?**

which is illustrated in Figure 11.3.

echo	character to toggle local echoing on/off
escape	character to escape back to telnet command mode
erase	character to cause an Erase Character
flushoutput	character to cause an Abort Output
interrupt	character to cause an Interrupt Process
kill	character to cause an Erase Line
quit	character to cause a Break
eof	character to cause an EOF
sak	character to cause remote host SAK sequence to be sent
?	character to display help information

Figure 11.2. telnet special character functions.

autoflush	toggle flushing of output when sending interrupt characters
autosynch	toggle automatic sending of interrupt characters in urgent mode
crmod	toggle mapping of received carriage returns
localchars	toggle local recognition of certain control characters
debug	toggle debugging output
netdata	toggle printing of hexadecimal network data for debugging
options	toggle viewing of options processing for debugging

Figure 11.3. telnet toggle options.

Another display of operating parameters can be obtained by entering the command

   telnet> **display**

the output of which is illustrated in Figure 11.4.

will flush output when sending interrupt characters.
won't send interrupt characters in urgent mode.
won't map carriage return on output.
won't recognize certain control characters.
won't turn on socket level debugging.
won't print hexadecimal representation of network traffic.
won't show option processing.

[^E]	echo.
[^T]	escape.
[^H]	erase.
[^O]	flushoutput.
[^C]	interrupt.
[^U]	kill.
[^\]	quit.
[^D]	eof.
[off]	sak.

Not emulating (native type vt220)

Figure 11.4. Display of current telnet operating parameters.

If you want to know the current condition of a connection to a remote host, you can execute the **status** command and the response would be:

Connected to hosta.company.com.
Operating in character-at-a-time mode.
Escape character is '^T'.

which indicates that a connection has been made to the remote host *hosta.company.com* and you are operating in the "character-at-a-time" mode.

Another level of help is available by using the command

telnet> **send** **?**

which is illustrated in Figure 11.5.

Send Option	What Option Does
ao	Send Telnet Abort output
ayt	Send Telnet 'Are You There'
brk	Send Telnet Break
ec	Send Telnet Erase Character
el	Send Telnet Erase Line
escape	Send current escape character
ga	Send Telnet 'Go Ahead' sequence
ip	Send Telnet Interrupt Process
nop	Send Telnet 'No operation'
sak	Send Telnet Secure Attention Key
synch	Perform Telnet 'Synch operation'

Figure 11.5. Available telnet send options.

For example, if you execute the **send ayt** while connected to a VMS system, you will get the response

RANCH::COWBOY   23:06:10   (DCL)   CPU=00:00:01.02
PF=537 IO=98   MEM=265

which indicates you are connected to a VMS system called *RANCH*. If you use the command **send ip**, you can interrupt the current process. If you send the command **send sak**, you will get the message: *Remote side does not support SAK*.

If you wanted to connect to the remote mail server on a remote host you would enter the **telnet** command followed by the "well-known" port number of the mail server, which is 25. These well-known port numbers can be found in the */etc/services* file (see Chapter 8 for further details). For example, the command

telnet   hostname   25

will cause the following output on your terminal:

Trying ...
Connected to hostname.
Escape character is "^]".
220 hostname Sendmail AIX 3.x/xxx xxx/xxx ready at xxx

indicating that you are connected to the mail server on *hostname*. You would now enter the commands that the "mail server" would use. (One way to find out the commands that the server recognizes is to enter the character "?" and usually the server will list the commands that it knows about.)

As another example, suppose you wanted to connect to the **ftp** server directly and not use the **ftp** command (see Chapter 15, Transferring Files, for more information on the **ftp** command). The well-known port number for the **ftp** server is 21. You would enter the command:

telnet   hostname   21

which would cause the following output on your terminal:

Trying ...
Connected to hostname.
Escape character is "^]".
220 hostname FTP server (Version xxx Date xxxxx) ready.

indicating that you are connected to the **FTP server** on *hostname*. You would now enter the commands that the "FTP server" would use.

Another method of connecting to various servers via the **telnet** command is to enter the **telnet** command by itself, as in

telnet

which will start the **telnet** command; you will get the following prompt on your terminal:

telnet>

You can now use the **open** command with the name of the host and port number that you want to connect with on the remote host as in the command

open   hostname   21

which will connect to the FTP server on *hostname.*

How the telnet Server Functions

The telnet command uses the TCP and IP protocols to establish communication with the remote server as illustrated in Figure 11.6. The telnet server listens at its assigned port number (23) until a request is received. When a request for a service is received, it performs negotiation of terminal characteristics and then starts a login session on the remote host. The process of negotiation requires exchange of a series of telnet messages until both ends of the telnet connection have agreed on services provided.

Telnet commands consist of at least a 2-byte sequence, the first byte of which is the command escape character (IAC) followed by the code that indicates what command is requested. All of the send functions shown in Table 11.1 and the special character operations shown in Table 11.2 are implemented using this form of telnet command. Table 11.3 shows what code value is used for each of the requested functions in Tables 11.1 and 11.2.

In addition, telnet commands are used to manage the negotiation process as well. Table 11.4 lists the various negotiation commands and what they mean. The "WILL, WON'T, DO, DON'T" methodology requires that one party to the telnet connection can send a WILL XXX command to indicate that they will begin to perform a particular option XXX. DO XXX and DON'T XXX indicate the other party's acceptance or rejection of that offer of service. DO XXX is a request that the other party perform service

XXX on the local system, and WILL XXX and WON'T XXX indicate agreement or not to provide that service. The network virtual terminal is the minimal set of services that telnet provides and the "WILL, WON'T, DO, and DON'T" sequence provides the abilities of both parties to agree on other mutually beneficial services to provide. It can be expected that at initial connection time, there will be a flurry of negotiation requests as each party requests additional services from the other. Once the negotiation process is complete, few negotiation requests will occur, but they can if either party wishes. Thus if a host implements a minimum set of telnet services, it can reject requests for other services without even understanding what services have been asked for.

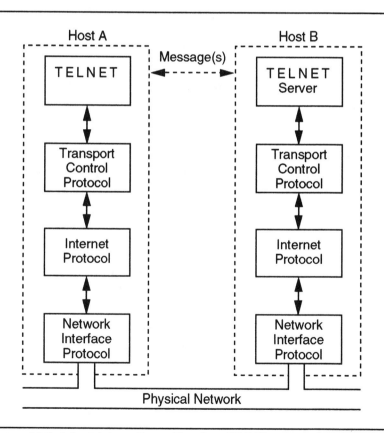

Figure 11.6. telnet interaction with other TCP/IP protocols.

Name	Code	What Code Does
NOP	241	No operation
Data Mark	242	The data stream portion of a Synch. This should always be accompanied by a TCP Urgent notification.
Break	243	NVT character BRK
Interrupt Process	244	The function IP
Abort output	245	The function AO
Are You There	246	The function AYT
Erase character	247	The function EC
Erase Line	248	The function EL
Go ahead	249	The GA signal
IAC	255	Data Byte 255

Table 11.3. Decimal code values for special telnet functions.

Negotiation rules include provisions that one party can even add a service temporarily if it wishes to and the other party agrees. Thus, for throughput reasons, it might be advantageous to offer some other services. In addition, negotiation rules require that one party can only request a change in status but not announce what status it is in. If an option is already on, the request is ignored.

Network Virtual Terminal

The Network Virtual Terminal (NVT) is an imaginary device that is used as a model for real terminals but that has a limited set of functions and a specified way of representing data. telnet hosts will emulate an NVT in conversing with each other. Thus the real terminal at which a telnet session has begun with its varied data representations will not be visible to the other end of a telnet connection. The translation of data to the format of the NVT is handled by the telnet process. A minimal set of functions is specified for the NVT so that even fairly modest terminals should be supportable. The two telnet partners can negotiate to add services to the minimal set the NVT has. If both partners can agree, some functions can be added.

Name	Code	What Code Does
SE	240	End of subnegotiation parameters.
SB	250	Indicates that what follows is subnegotiation of the indicated option.
WILL (option code)	251	Indicates the desire to begin performing, or confirmation that you are now performing, the indicated option.
WON'T (option code)	252	Indicates the refusal to perform, or continue performing, the indicated option.
DO (option code)	253	Indicates the request that the other party perform, or confirmation that you are expecting the other party to perform, the indicated option.
DON'T (option code)	254	Indicates the demand that the other party stop performing, or confirmation that you are no longer expecting the other party to perform, the indicated option.

Table 11.4. Decimal code values for telnet negotiation commands.

The NVT is a bidirectional, character-based device with a printer and a keyboard. Incoming data is sent to the printer and outgoing data comes from the keyboard. Echoing commands means echoing the command locally since it would not be wise to send echoes through the network. The code set supported is 7-bit ASCII characters transmitted in 8-bit bytes. The NVT appears to be half-duplex even though telnet sessions are inherently full duplex. This choice was made to keep the cost of managing data through a telnet session to a minimum, requiring few data buffers. After the process has finished sending data to the printer and has no queued input from the NVT keyboard, the process must issue the telnet Go Ahead (GA) command to turn the line around. This requirement is due to the way the initial terminal (an IBM 2741 terminal) operated in that it locked its keyboard after sending its output and waited for its keyboard to be unlocked before allowing more input.

The code set for the NVT includes representations of all 95 ASCII graphics including upper- and lowercase characters, numbers, punctuation, and so forth. Of the 33 ASCII control codes less than 127, Table 11.5 lists those that cause the NVT printer to perform some special function. As shown earlier in Tables 11.3 and 11.4, a number of codes above 128 have special meanings.

Character Name	Code	Meaning
Null (NUL)	0	No Operation
Line Feed (LF)	10	Moves the printer to the next print line, keeping the same horizontal position.
Carriage Return (CR)	13	Moves the printer to the left margin of the current line.
Bell (BEL)	7	Produces an audible or visible signal (which does NOT move the print head).
Back Space (BS)	8	Moves the print head one character position toward the left margin.
Horizontal Tab (HT)	9	Moves the printer to the next horizontal tab stop. It remains unspecified how either party determines or establishes where such tab stops are located.
Vertical Tab (VT)	11	Moves the printer to the next vertical tab stop. It remains unspecified how either party determines or establishes where such tab stops are located.
Form Feed (FF)	12	Moves the printer to the top of the next page, keeping the same horizontal position.

Note: All remaining codes do not cause the NVT printer to take any action.

Table 11.5. Special codes for the NVT printer.

Summary

Establishing a session on a remote host (even a dissimilar one) to interactively execute commands can be performed by executing the telnet command. Dissimilar systems can be connected to because telnet uses a model of an ASCII terminal (called the Network Virtual Terminal) and all data is transmitted as if from such a terminal. telnet commands can be used to connect to any of the TCP/IP servers on remote hosts.

Manual pages that describe how the telnet command operates form the basis for the operational examples that illustrate how users use telnet.

Much of the theoretical discussion in this chapter is based on the RFC that describes the telnet process: J. Postel and J. Reynolds, "telnet Protocol Specification," RFC 854 (1981). A set of RFCs that describe in detail how many of the individual telnet functions operate are listed in Table A.4 in Appendix A.

12

Copying Files from Host to Host (rcp Command)

Introduction

The Remote Copy (**rcp**) command is used to copy a file (or files) from one host ("source") to another host ("destination"). Either of these hosts may be local to the host that the command is executed from. In addition, the **rcp** command can be used to copy directory trees from one host to another. For flexibility you can specify the names of users on either host.

This chapter will examine how to use the **rcp** command, how the server that supports the **rcp** command operates, and what problems can occur when executing rcp commands.

How to Use the rcp Command

In order to perform the simplest of **rcp** commands, to copy a file from one host to another you would use the syntax

    rcp   file1   host1:file2

which will copy the contents of *file1* that is on the local host to the remote host *host1* and call it *file2*. Alternatively, if *file1* is on a remote host (*host1*) and you wish to copy it to your local host and call it *file2*, you would use

    rcp   host1:file1   file2

If the name of the file on the local host will be the same at the name of the file on the remote host, the specification of the name on the local host can be replaced with a period (.). Thus

rcp   host1:file1 .

will copy *file1* from the remote host *host1* to the local host as *file1*. If the file you want to copy is not on the local host but on a remote host (*host1*) and you want to copy it to a remote host (*host2*), you would use

rcp   host1:file1   host2:file2

which would copy *file1* on *host1* to *file2* on *host2*.

If the name of a directory is used as the destination instead of the name of a file, the source file is copied into the destination directory and keeps its original name. Thus

rcp   file1   host2:directory2

indicates that *file1* will be copied to *directory2* on *host2*. Also, it is possible to list several files that are to be copied into the directory, for example, as in the following command:

rcp   file1   file2   file3   host2:directory2

which will cause *file1*, *file2*, and *file3* to all be copied into *directory2* on host *host2*. If the path of the destination file or directory is not fully qualified (that is to say, does not begin with a /), the path is interpreted as beginning at the home directory of the remote user account, which will be the same as the local user account unless otherwise specified.

If metacharacters such as *, $, and so forth are included in the file name or the directory name, and these need to be interpreted on the remote host and not on the local host, they must be enclosed in " (double quotes), ' (single quotes), or preceded by a \ (backslash) so that the local shell will not interpret them.

For all of the above cases, the user name from the local host is used on both the local host and on the remote host. However, it is possible to override that assumption by specifying the name of the user on either the local host or on the remote host by using

rcp   file1   user1@host1:file2

which would copy *file1* (under the local user's name) to *file1* on *host1* under the name of the user *user1*. On the remote host *user1* must have created a file to grant permission to another user to access *user1's* files. This file (**.rhosts** file) is described in detail in Chapter 8. Some implementations of this command require a slightly different format for this command. On those systems, the previous command would be specified

rcp   file1   user1.host1:file2

which would copy *file1* onto *host1* and call it *file2*.

If you are copying files from one remote host to another, you can specify two different user names if you wish, as in the following:

rcp   user1@host1:file1   user2@host2:file2

which would copy file1 on *host1* as *user1'* to *file2* to *host2* as *user2*. Here again, some UNIX implementations have a different syntax, and this previous command would then be

rcp   user1.host1:file1   user2.host2:file2

If the destination file exists, its permissions and ownership will be preserved. If the destination file does not exist, the file permissions and ownership will be the same as the source file. If you wish to preserve the modification time of a file, use a special option (-p) when you perform the **rcp** command.

One last function that the rcp command can perform is to copy an entire directory tree (with all of the files in it) from one host to another by specifying the names of the source directory and destination directory, as in

rcp   host1:directory1   host2:directory2

which will copy the contents of the *directory1* on *host1* to *directory2* on *host2*. If the specification of either *host1* or *host2* or both is left out, the operation will work the same, with the local host being used as the source or destination. If there are subdirectories in the source directory, it will not be copied unless you add the -r (recursive) flag to your **rcp** command. Thus the following will copy all of the files and all of the subdirectories in *directory1* to *directory2* on *host2*:

    rcp   -r   directory1   host2:directory2

For both the source directory and destination directory, the user can be specified. If the name of either or both of the directories are not fully qualified, the home directory of the user is added. Specifying the user to operate as on a remote node means specifying a different home directory.

How the rcp Server Validates the rcp Command

The **rcp** command uses the user name entered for the remote host to determine file access privileges at the remote host. But before that can happen, the **rcp** command determines if it has access to the remote host by determining that the name of the local host is in the remote host's */etc/hosts.equiv* file.

The second level of validation is that the user under which the remote copy operation is being done is defined on the remote host. The **rcp** command will permit the copy operation even if the remote user has no password. (Some remote operations require that the user have a password or the operation will be invalidated.)

The third level is to check whether access to the remote user's directories are permitted by examining the *.rhosts* file in the home directory of the remote user. This file needs to contain entries that specify the remote host and user name. Only those users on those hosts will be able to remotely access this directory. If the *.rhosts* file does not exist, the copy command will fail if the user does not have access to the remote user's directories. If the user name is specified for the remote host, that user's name is used to set ownership and determines file access privileges that the **rcp** command will use at that host.

What Problems Can Occur with the rcp Command

Most of the problems that commonly occur while using the **rcp** command are due to the nonexistence of either the file to be copied, the directory to be copied to or from, or the name of the host. When copying from one host to another, the following are some of the error messages that can occur.

host: name —— —— *not found or* —— ——*: host not found*

means that the host name that has been specified is not known to the local host. Usually this is due to the absence of the remote host's name in the */etc/hosts* file.

rcp: — ——*: not a plain file*

means that the form of the **rcp** command that was used required the name of a file and the entry given was not a file (but was probably a directory instead).

rcp: invalid user name — —— *or*
rcp: — —— *does not have an account on this machine*

indicates that the user name that you are using on the remote host is not known on that remote host.

Permission denied.

indicates that one of the tests that the **rshd** performed failed. Often the message starts with

rsh server:

and indicates that either the user does not exist or does not have access privileges to the user's directory.

How the rcp Server Functions

Both the **rcp** and the **rsh** commands are serviced by the **rshd** server (or daemon). This server provides for the remote execution of shell commands for the **rsh** command or the execution of the copy command for **rcp** command. The server operates by listening at the port number defined in the */etc/services* file.

Requests for service arrive at that port from remote hosts ("clients"), as shown in Figure 12.1.

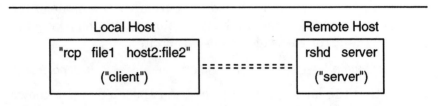

Figure 12.1. rcp command and its rshd server process.

When a request for service arrives, the server must validate that the request comes from an appropriate client on an appropriate host and is properly formulated. There are several steps that the server follows to ensure that it is a proper request.

When the server receives a service request, the server does the following:

1. The server checks the source port number of the client that made the request. If the port number is not in the range 0 to 1023, that is, one of the port numbers reserved for system functions, the request is denied.

2. The server then reads characters from the socket up to a null byte and uses that number as the port number of a secondary port to use for standard error output. The server then establishes a second connection with the client's host using the port number it has just read.

3. The server then reads from the socket the name of the user on the client host, the name of the user on the server host, and the command to be executed. The name of the user on the local server is validated in the /etc/passwd file, and the home directory of the user is determined. The current working directory is changed to the home directory of the user. If either the lookup of the user's name or the change to the user's home directory fails, the service request is discarded.

4. The name of the client host is looked up in the */etc/hosts.equiv* file and, if it doesn't exist, the request will be discarded.

5. If the *.rhosts* file exists in the home directory of the user, the requesting user is looked up in that file. If this fails, the request is denied.

Once all of these validations have been performed, the command is then passed to the user's login shell. The command(s) are then processed and the interaction between the requesting process and the **rshd** server proceeds, as illustrated in Figure 12.2.

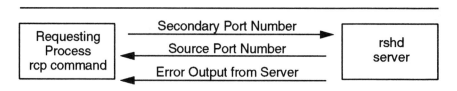

Figure 12.2. Establishing connection between rcp command and rshd server.

As indicated in this outline, the error messages can be processed and returned to the requesting process without disrupting the copy process.

Summary

The copying of files from one host to another can be most easily accomplished using the **rcp** command.

Manual pages that are found on most UNIX systems form the basis for the discussion of the various options available with the **rcp** command.

13

Executing Commands on a Remote Host (rsh Command)

Introduction

The **rsh** command is used to execute a command on a remote host. Any command for which the user has authority can be executed on a remote host. The output from such a command (if there is any) will be returned to the local host as if the command had been executed on the local host. If no command is specified, the user is logged into the remote host.

This chapter will examine how to use the **rsh** command, how the server that supports the **rsh** command operates, and what problems can occur when executing **rsh** commands.

Executing Single Commands on a Remote Host

Sometimes running just *one* command on a remote host is all that is needed. For example, checking whether a user is defined on a remote host can be done with a single command that is executed on the remote host. Or, as another example, suppose a user wanted to determine what time a remote host believes it to be. Checking the time on another host doesn't require a user to login; it requires that a single command be executed on the remote host itself and the output of the command be returned to the originating host. As another example, the current processing load on a remote host could be checked, and if it is low, users might choose to execute their operations on that host rather than on the one to which they are locally attached.

Earlier chapters described how to establish a session on a remote host in order to execute commands on that host. This process of logging in requires executing a command that does not return any information to the user but only establishes a connection so that future commands can be executed on the remote host. But in many cases the information that the user desires or the operation that the user wants to execute are one-step operations. In these cases the logging-in operation is wasted. For these cases, executing individual commands without logging in may be more efficient for users.

How to Use the rsh Command

To run single commands on a remote host, the syntax for the **rsh** command is:

> **rsh   RemoteHost   CommandName**

which will execute the command **CommandName** on the remote host *RemoteHost*. For example, the command

> **rsh   host1   df**

will request the amount of available free disk space on remote host *host1*.

Almost any command can be executed on the remote host. If the command is not allowed because the user does not have the privilege to execute the command, the command will be rejected by the remote host. The **rsh** server executes the requested command under the user id of the user on the local host who requested the command. The commands are executed on the remote host using the HOME directory of the user (as defined in the */etc/ passwd* file on the remote host). Thus files that do not have an absolute path specified for them will be searched for in the HOME directory of the user on the remote host. For example,

> **rsh   host1   cp   file1   file2**

will look for *file1* in the home directory of the user on the remote host and will copy its contents to *file2* in the home directory on the remote host *host1*.

To execute a command under a different user name, use the -i option on the command line following the name of the remote host. The following command will execute the **cat /etc/ passwd** command under the user id *tom*:

rsh   host1   -i   tom   cat /etc/passwd

A different user id might be needed if the local user does not have the necessary level of privilege on the remote host or is not even known on the remote host.

Output generated by the **rsh** command can be stored in a local file. The command

rsh   host1   cat file1   >>   file2

will append the contents of *file1* from the remote host to the current contents of *file2* on the local host if it exists and, if it does not, will create *file2* and fill it with the contents of *file1*. The output of the **cat** command ends up on the local host because the "shell" command on the local host will interpret the >> as a request for the local host to execute. If appending the contents of one remote file to the current contents of another *remote* file is desired, the redirection operation >> will need to be shielded from the local shell by using quotation marks ("). The command

rsh   host1   cat file1   ">>"   file2

will append the contents of *file1* on the remote host *host1* to the current contents of *file2* on the remote host. This entire command occurs exclusively on the remote host.

More than one command can be executed on the remote host using the ";" operator. But since the metacharacter ";" will be interpreted by the local shell, the whole string of commands must be enclosed in quotation marks. For example, the command

rsh   host1   "cd lowerdir;cat test2   >>   test3"

will perform the concatenation operation in the subdirectory *lowerdir* of the HOME directory of the user on the remote host *host1*. But the command

    rsh   host1   cd lowerdir;cat test2 >> test3

will perform the concatenation operation in the current directory of the user on the local host, and the specification of the **cd** command will be wasted.

Any output generated by the remote command is sent back to the local host. If the output cannot be displayed because the **rsh** command is being executed in the background, the rsh command will be suspended. If the command is to be executed in the background, a special flag (-n) can be used to send the output to the "bit bucket" */dev/null*; otherwise the command will halt when the first output is generated. Thus the command

    rsh   host1   -n   cat /etc/hosts

will execute the command on the remote host *host1* but no output will be shown on the local host.

If the **rsh** command is executed by itself with only the name of the remote host on the command line, as in the following:

    rsh   host1

the **rlogin** command will be executed and a login into the remote host will be attempted. In addition, a set of aliases for the **/usr/ucb/rsh** executable can be created by executing commands such as

    ln   -s   /usr/ucb/rsh   RemoteHost1

Then, when you enter just the name of the remote host of interest, such as

    RemoteHost1

the actual command that is executed is

    rsh RemoteHost1

and the user will be logged automatically into *RemoteHost1*.

Once you have the aliases defined, you can execute a command on a remote host just by entering the name of the host, for example, masterhost, and the command you want to execute on it. For example,

masterhost   date

will execute the date command on the host masterhost.

The **rsh** command connects the standard input from the local command line as standard input to the remote command. Input that is generated by one command can be piped using the pipeline (|) operation into an **rsh** command and have that generated output as input to the execution of the command on the remote host. Thus the following command, using a pipeline operation,

tar cvf - . | rsh host1 tar xvf -

will create a tar output file on the local host on standard output, which is in turn tied to standard input for the tar command being run on the remote host host1. This command has the effect of copying files from one directory on one host into a directory on another host.

While the command on the remote host is executing, a user can interrupt the processing or cause it to halt by entering the appropriate control character sequence. When the remote command terminates, the local rsh command will also terminate.

Interactive commands cannot be executed using an **rsh** command because input to the command must be specified on the command line.

Unlike some other remote commands such as **ftp**, the **rsh** command can be executed using a user id that has no password. Unfortunately, setting up such users violates the security of a system and is usually not done.

In some UNIX implementations, the command to execute single commands on a remote host may not be **rsh**, but instead may be **rcmd** (SCO UNIX), or **remsh** (HP-UX). Examination of the manual pages for the UNIX system of interest should provide the name of the command to use.

How the rsh Server Functions

The validation that the **rsh** server does is the same as the validation that is performed for the **rcp** command. In fact, the **rsh** server (normally called rshd) services both the **rsh** and **rcp** commands.

The remote host allows access only if at least one of the following conditions is true:

1. The local user is not the root user, and the name of the local host is listed as an equivalent host in the /etc/hosts.equiv file on the remote system.

2. The remote user's home directory (as defined in the /etc/ passwd file) contains an .rhosts file that lists the local host and the local user name. For security reasons, the .rhosts file must be read by either the remote user or root, and only the owner should have read and write access. In some implementations, if the permissions on the .rhosts file are not read/ write only by owner, the file will be ignored and the request will be rejected.

In addition to the above, the **rsh** server validates the port number of the requesting process to ensure that it is a system request.

Standard error is transmitted back to the local host over a separate connection between the local host and the remote host.

What Problems Can Occur with the rsh Command

Output from a command executed on the remote system will be sent back to the local host. If this command is executed in a background mode, the remote command will halt if the command cannot write its output onto a terminal.

Special characters such as redirection (>>) or metacharacters such as * . { , } and so forth that have meaning to the various shell programs will be interpreted on the local system and not on the remote system as desired. The user needs to make sure that these special characters are interpreted and acted upon on the particular host that the user has in mind. If the user wants these special characters to be interpreted on the local host, nothing needs to be done. If the user wants these special characters to be interpreted on the remote host, they need to be enclosed in quotation marks (").

The local user may not be known on the remote system. This type of problem will lead to the user being denied access to the remote system. One approach to this problem is to use the -i option to specify the name of a user who is known on the remote system.

The local host may not be properly defined on the remote system in the various network tables. This error will result in the local system being denied access to the remote system.

Summary

Executing single commands on a remote host without logging in can be performed by using the **rsh** command. Any valid command that the user has the privilege to execute on the remote system can be run. Output from the command is returned to the originating host. One option allows the specification of a user name different from the user name on the local host.

For further information on the **rsh** command or the **rshd** server, the user can examine the manual pages on the particular UNIX system of interest.

14

Simple File Transfer (tftp Command)

Introduction

Transferring single files between hosts of possibly dissimilar file systems (such as UNIX and VMS) can be accomplished using the **tftp** command. The **tftp** command is only meant for transferring one file at a time and does not provide many of the features that the **ftp** command provides (described in the next chapter). For example, **tftp** does not support listing remote files or changing directories at the remote host site. **tftp** uses UDP as its transport protocol, which while providing less services, simplifies the implementation of the command. Thus **tftp** services are suitable for loading diskless workstations.

This chapter will examine how to use the **tftp** command, how the server that supports the **tftp** command operates, and what problems can occur when executing **tftp** commands.

How to Use the tftp Command

The commands can be used in two different forms: interactive form and command line form. In command line form, all of the options for either command can be specified on the command line.

The **tftp** command uses the UDP protocol and not the TCP protocol. tftp does form a connection to the remote host, but only for the duration of the transfer. In addition, there is no authentication of whether the request the **tftp** command is making is valid for this user or not. This command is suitable for downloading diskless workstations because all that needs to be known is the address of the host to download (the port is "well-known").

When data is transferred to a remote host, the transferred data is placed in the directory specified by the RemoteName parameter, which must be a fully specified file name; the remote file must both exist and have write permissions set for others.

The command line format provides command line flags to specify all of the various functions that you can use. The **tftp** command with its options is described in Figure 14.1. One note: if the file already exits on the local host, the **tftp** command will prompt before overwriting the already existing file.

---

tftp {-w or -p or -r or -g} LocalName Host Port RemoteName
                                                    {transfer type}

where:

-w or -p	indicates that the local file will be written to the Remote Name
-r or -g	indicates that the contents of RemoteName will be read from the remote host and written to LocaName
LocalName	name of the file to read data into or write data from
Host	name of the remote host to communicate with
Port	port number to use on the remote host
RemoteName	name of the file to write data into or read data from
{transfer type}	specifies whether data is 7-bit ASCII-like or 8-bit Binary

---

Figure 14.1. tftp command and its options.

Some Examples of Use of the tftp Command

Copying a file from one system to another is the main use of the **tftp** command. For example, the command

tftp -g newbook1 host1 /u/fred/book1

will copy file */u/fred/book1* on host *host1* to the local host and save it as *newbook1*.

You can specify a - (dash) as the LocalName, and then when reading from a remote host the output will be written to standard output. For example,

tftp -g - host5 /etc/hosts

will display on your terminal the contents of the */etc/hosts* file from the remote host *host5*.

You can specify a - (dash) as the LocalName, and then when writing to a remote host, the tftp command will read input from standard input to be sent to the remote host.

Output from the **tftp** command can be piped into another command. For example, suppose you want to check that *host9* is defined in the */etc/hosts* file on *host8*. The following command would do that:

tftp -g - host8 /etc/hosts | grep host9

You can copy a file onto another system with

tftp -p /u/fred/test host2 /tmp/test

which will copy file */u/fred/test* onto *host2* as file */tmp/test*.

In the interactive mode, all of the various reading and writing functions can be used; reading and writing files is requested via the **get** and **put** commands. To enter interactive mode, issue the command

tftp

and, once you do that, the interactive prompt

tftp>

is displayed. The hostname can be specified in the **get** or **put** command. For example:

tftp> **get host5:/etc/hosts /tmp/hosts**

will copy from *host5* the */etc/hosts* file and save it on the local host as */tmp/hosts*. Or, the following

tftp> **put /etc/hosts host5:/etc/hosts**

will replace */etc/hosts* file on *host5*. While in the interactive mode, you can use the status command to determine which host you will be accessing.

What Problems Can Occur With the tftp Command

Because this is a simple command, there are only a few possible errors that can occur; they are listed with the error code and an explanation of the error in Table 14.1. All of these error codes are fatal and will cause the transfer to be terminated. In addition, the error packet is not acknowledged or retransmitted and may not be received. In any event, no further transmissions will take place.

Error Code	Error Message	Meaning of Error Message
0	Not Defined	Look at error message for explanation
1	File Not Found	File name is not valid
2	Access Violation	Denied access to file
3	Disk Full	No room on disk for file
4	Illegal tftp Operation	
5	Unknown Port Number	
6	File Already Exists	tftp will not overwrite a file that already exists
7	No Such User	User's name not known to remote system

Table 14.1. Possible error codes during tftp transfers.

How the tftp Server Functions

The **tftp** command used UDP as its protocol because it is connectionless. As shown in Figure 14.2, the tftp command acts as a "client" process and communicates with the tftp server on the remote host to request the service desired. The connection is only for the duration of the data exchange. Any error will cause the connection to be closed.

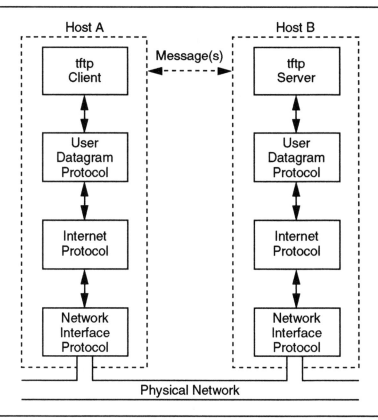

Figure 14.2. tftp interaction with other TCP/IP protocols.

How the tftp Protocol Works

The five types of message packets are illustrated in Figure 14.3. The READ REQUEST and WRITE REQUEST packets contain a file name in ASCII text (terminated with \000) that is the name of the file to transfer. In addition, this packet also contains the format specifier "octet" or "netascii" in the mode field. This packet is used to initiate the transfer of data and must be the first packet sent.

The DATA packet contains the block of data being transferred and includes a Block Number. Each packet contains exactly 512 bytes except for the last block, which must contain less than 512 bytes. A packet that contains less than 512 bytes is the last block in the file and initiates the disconnect sequence.

The ACKNOWLEDGMENT packet acknowledges the receipt of a block and contains the number of the block which it is acknowledging. The numbering of blocks is sequential, and the first block of data transferred is block number 1. Each block must be successfully acknowledged before another block will be sent.

The ERROR packet contains the error code and optional message indicating the error condition.

The connection to the remote host is initiated by sending the READ REQUEST or WRITE REQUEST to the well-known port address (69) of the tftp server on the remote host. The port number of the requester is chosen by the requesting process and should be randomized to avoid using the same port numbers in immediate succession.

When the tftp server on the remote host receives the request, it will choose a new port number for itself, again in random sequence. Thus the well-known port number for the tftp server is freed up so that another request can be serviced. The UDP packet contains the port number that the requesting process has chosen so that a reply to that process can be sent correctly addressed. The first reply to the initial request contains the port number to which all subsequent data packets (or acknowledgments for a write request) should be sent. Thus the port number of the tftp server is used for sending requests and two other ports are used for the actual data transfer that has been requested. Each receipt of another packet must be checked to be sure that the correct port number sent that packet, since port numbers are being used randomly and are not reserved for just the tftp requests. When the last block has been received and acknowledged, the connection can be terminated.

Type of Message	Layout of Message					
	2 Bytes	String	1 Byte	String	1 Byte	
READ REQUEST (RRQ)	01	Name of File	0	Mode	0	
	2 Bytes	String	1 Byte	String	1 Byte	
WRITE REQUEST (WRQ)	02	Name of File	0	Mode	0	
	2 Bytes	2 Bytes	Up to 512 Bytes			
DATA	03	Block #	Data			
	2 Bytes	2 Bytes				
ACK	04	Block #				
	2 Bytes	2 Bytes	String	1 Byte		
ERROR	05	ErrorCode	Error Message	0		

Figure 14.3. Different tftp message types.

A transfer is started by sending a write request (WRQ) to write a file or a read request (RRQ) to read a file to a remote system. Receiving an acknowledgment packet as a reply to the write request or receiving a data packet as a reply to a read request are both positive acknowledgments, as illustrated in Figures 14.4 and 14.5. Each data packet that is received correctly is acknowledged with an acknowledgment packet that contains the block number. The block numbering is consecutive and starts with 1. Each block of data contains exactly 512 bytes except for the last block. Every data block must be successfully acknowledged before another one will be sent. Thus only one data block will need to be retransmitted if there is an error. The last block of data in a transfer is recognized because it contains less than 512 bytes.

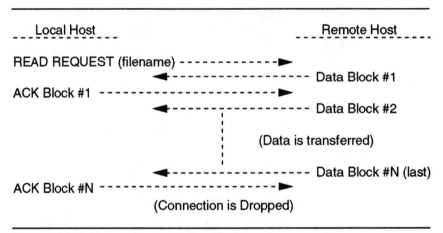

Figure 14.4. Using tftp to read a file.

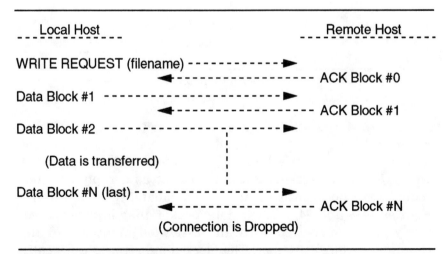

Figure 14.5. Using tftp to write a file.

Two error conditions can occur and each needs to be dealt with for the transfer to succeed: no receipt of a data packet or an acknowledgment within the expected time period, and receipt of an acknowledgment with an invalid block number. Figure 14.6 illustrates that if a timeout occurs, the last transmission is re-sent, and Figure 14.7 shows that if an invalid block number is acknowledged (indicating that the last data block was not received), the correct data block is sent. No ambiguity about which data block needs to be sent can occur since only one data block can be unacknowledged at any time.

Closing a connection has no particular sequence of responses. When the transfer is done, the connection will be closed. The tftp server can drop the connection as soon as the last block is sent, although it should wait for the last acknowledgment to be received. The tftp requester does not know that the acknowledgment was received, but so long as it successfully received all of the blocks in the file, it will not matter if the acknowledgment is received by the tftp server.

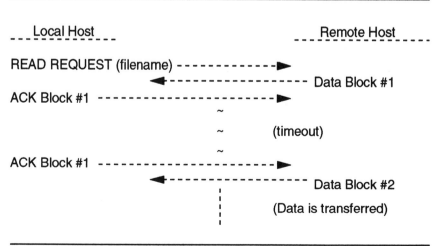

Figure 14.6. Recovery after timeout during tftp read request.

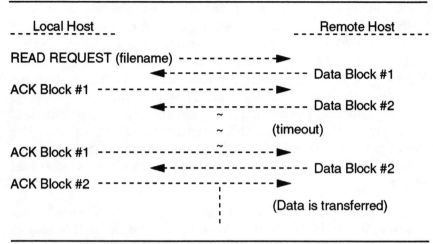

Figure 14.7. Recovery after bad acknowledgment during tftp read request.

Summary

The **tftp** command is a simple file transfer command that can be used to down load diskless workstations. Only reading and writing of files are supported functions.

For further information on the **tftp** command, examine the manual page that is available on your favorite UNIX system. For more information on the tftp protocol, look at RFC 1350.

15

Transferring Files Between Hosts (ftp Command)

Introduction

The File Transfer (**ftp**) command is used to transfer files between hosts of possibly dissimilar file systems (such as UNIX versus VMS). Any kind of file can be transferred. One restriction that ftp imposes is that the user that is executing the **ftp** command must be known to the remote host and must have a password defined for it. (Some systems allow the use of the user "anonymous," which might not have a password and provide a special area for files that this user can access.) Thus the use of the ftp command is fairly secure even though any readable file on a system can be retrieved by the **ftp** command.

The **ftp** command operates in an interactive mode, which involves the user establishing a connection with the ftp server on the remote system using the TCP protocol. FTP establishes two connections between the client and the server, one for control information such as commands and responses, and a second for transferring data. The interactive user will be prompted for a user name and password to establish the connection with the remote system. Once the connection is established, both text and binary files can be transferred.

This chapter will examine how to use the **ftp** command, how the server that supports the **ftp** command operates, and what problems can occur when executing **ftp** commands.

How to Use the ftp Command

The **ftp** command provides a rich set of file manipulation commands, which can be grouped into the following categories:

Transferring and managing files

Changing and listing contents of directories

Managing which files will be transferred

Managing connections with remote hosts

Managing the characteristics of files being transferred

Managing what prompting occurs and miscellaneous operations

Writing macros to group commands into supercommands

Each of these groups of commands will be addressed in the following sections. One note when specifying these commands: any part of the command that is enclosed in [] (brackets) is optional.

Transferring Files and Managing Files

Since one of the major functions of the **ftp** command is to transfer files, this command provides a large number of commands to facilitate transferring and managing the files that were transferred. (Note that the naming of files on the local host and remote hosts is affected by the setting of the ntrans and nmap options.) These commands are summarized in Table 15.1.

- **append LocalFile [RemoteFile]** will transfer *LocalFile* to the remote system and will add its contents to the current contents of *RemoteFile* if it is specified and exists or will add its contents to the *LocalFile* (on the remote system) if it exists. If neither *RemoteFile* is specified nor does *LocalFile* exist, *LocalFile* will be created and will contain whatever *LocalFile* contained on the local host.

- **delete RemoteFile** will delete the file named *RemoteFile* on the remote system if it exists.

ftp Command			Action
append	**LocalFile**	**[RemoteFile]**	Add contents of LocalFile to RemoteFile
delete	**RemoteFile**		Delete RemoteFile
get	**RemoteFile**	**[LocalFile]**	Retrieve contents of RemoteFile
mdelete	**RemoteFiles**		Delete RemoteFile(s)
mget	**RemoteFiles**		Retrieve contents of RemoteFile(s)
mput	**[LocalFiles]**		Transfer Contents of LocalFile(s)
put	**LocalFile**	**[RemoteFile]**	Transfer LocalFile
recv	**RemoteFile**	**[LocalFile]**	Retrieve contents of RemoteFile
rename	**FromName**	**ToName**	Rename File on Remote System
send	**LocalFile**	**[RemoteFile]**	Transfer LocalFile

Table 15.1. **ftp** commands to transfer and manage files.

- **get RemoteFile [LocalFile]** and **recv RemoteFile [LocalFile]** will transfer the file *RemoteFile* from the remote host to the local host and will name that file *LocalFile* if *LocalFile* has been specified or *RemoteFile* if *LocalFile* was not specified.

- **mdelete RemoteFiles** will delete the group of files whose names are generated by the expansion of the *RemoteFiles* specification.

- **mget RemoteFiles** will transfer the set of files specified by *RemoteFiles* from the remote host to the local host and retain their original names on the local host. Usually the specification RemoteFiles contains special characters to indicate what group of files is intended to be transferred. These special characters such as * , { and so forth, are often called metacharacters and are interpreted just as the C shell would.

- **mput [LocalFiles]** will transfer the group of LocalFiles to the remote host and name them the same as modified by the setting of ntrans and nmap options.

- **put LocalFile [RemoteFile]** and **send LocalFile [RemoteFile]** will transfer the contents of file named *LocalFile* from the local system to the remote system and will name the file *RemoteFile* if a name is specified or will name the file *LocalFile* if *RemoteFile* is not specified. The file name on the remote host will be modified by the setting of ntrans and nmap options.

- **rename FromName ToName** will rename the file named *FromName* to a file named *ToName* on the remote system.

Listing and Changing Directories

The following commands are for managing the directory to which you are transferring files or from which you are transferring files. Table 15.2 summarizes how these commands operate.

- **cd RemoteDirectory** will change the current working directory on the remote system to be *RemoteDirectory*.

- **cdup** will move up one level in the directory tree on the remote system.

- **dir [RemoteDirectory] [LocalFile]** or **ls [Remote-Directory] [LocalFile]** writes a listing of the contents of the *RemoteDirectory* into *LocalFile* on the local host. If the *LocalFile* is not specified, the listing of the contents of the *RemoteDirectory* are displayed on the local terminal. If the *RemoteDirectory* is not specified, a listing of the current directory is displayed on the local terminal.

- **lcd [Directory]** changes the working directory on the local host to *Directory*.

- **mdir [RemoteDirectories LocalFile]** or **mls [RemoteDirectories LocalFile]** writes a listing of the contents of the set of directories to which *RemoteDirectories* expands to the *LocalFile* file if it is specified or to the local terminal if *LocalFile* is a hyphen (-). If *LocalFile* is not specified, the name of a local file will be prompted for. *RemoteDirectories* may contain metacharacters and/or pattern-matching characters. *RemoteDirectories* may contain a list of remote directories separated by blanks.

- **mkdir RemoteDirectory** will create the directory *RemoteDirectory* on the remote host.

- **nlist** prints a list of the files of a directory on the remote host

- **pwd** displays the name of the current directory on the remote host.

- **rmdir RemoteDirectory** removes the directory *RemoteDirectory* from the remote host.

- **size Filename** returns the size of *Filename* on the remote machine in bytes.

ftp Command		Action
lcd	**[Directory]**	Changes local working directory
mdir	**[RemoteDirectories LocalFile]**	Lists contents of *RemoteDirectories* into *LocalFile*
mkdir	**RemoteDirectory**	Creates the directory *RemoteDirectory*
mls	**[RemoteDirectories LocalFile]**	Lists contents of *RemoteDirectories* into *LocalFile*
nlist		Lists contents of a directory
pwd		Displays the name of the current directory
rmdir	**RemoteDirectory**	Removes the directory *RemoteDirectory*
size	**Filename**	Returns the size of *Filename*

Table 15.2. **ftp** commands to change and list directories.

Managing Which File(s) Will Be Transferred

Often it is desired to transfer a group of files, and it would be an advantage to be able to specify a group of files to be transferred. In addition, when transferring files between two dissimilar file systems it may be important to modify the name of the transferred files to fit the syntax of the target system. The following commands (summarized in Table 15.3) enable the user to specify some naming options. These options can be used to adjust the names of files that are being transferred from systems that use only uppercase file names to those that can use lowercase names. Furthermore, on some systems, file extensions may have different meanings and this needs to be changed on the receiving system.

- **case** is a toggle that, when it is on, will cause remote file names that are displayed in uppercase letters to be changed to lowercase letters when these files are created on the local system.

- **glob** is a toggle that, when it is on, will cause the expansion of filenames for the **mget**, **mput**, and **mdelete** commands and when it is off, will suppress expansion of file names.

- **nmap [InPattern OutPattern]** enables file name mapping with any occurrence of *InPattern* changed to *OutPattern*. This option can be used to specify the naming of destination files during **mput** or **put** operations or source files during **mget** or **get** operations.

- **ntrans [InCharacter [OutCharacter]]** enables file name character translation with *InCharacter(s)* replaced by *OutCharacter(s)* for source file names or destination file names.

- **runique** causes unique file names to be created for local destination files during **get** and **mget** subcommands. If a local destination file name already exists, a unique name will be created, adding .1 to the usual destination file name. If that name already exists, the number is incremented until a unique name is generated.

- **sunique** causes unique file names to be created for remote destination files during **put** and **mput** subcommands.
If a remote destination file name already exists, a unique
name will be created, adding .1 to the usual destination
file name. If that name already exists, the number is
incremented until a unique name is generated.

ftp Command	Action
case	Convert file names to lowercase (or not)
glob	Expand file names (or not)
nmap [InPattern OutPattern]	Map file names using patterns
ntrans [InCharacter [OutCharacter]]	Translate file names
runique	Create unique file names during **get** or **mget** operations (or not)
sunique	Create unique file names during **put** or **mput** operations (or not)

Table 15.3. **ftp** commands to manage which files will be transferred.

Managing Passwords

The **ftp** command provides a number of ways to control which
remote host you are connected to and what your user name and
password for that remote host might be. These commands are
summarized in Table 15.4.

- **account [Password]** sends a supplemental password that
a remote host may require before allowing access to certain resources.

- **bye** or **quit** ends the ftp session and exits the command.

- **close** or **disconnect** ends the ftp session but does not exit
the **ftp** command. The ftp prompt will be displayed next.

- **open HostName [Port]** establishes a connection to the ftp server on *HostName*. If the *Port* is specified, the connection to a server will be at that port. If autologin is set, the ftp command will attempt to automatically log the user into the ftp server. (The file *.netrc* must exist in the user's home directory with the correct information before autologin will succeed.)

- **sendport** is a toggle that controls the use of PORT ftp command.

- **user User [Password] [Account]** identifies the local user as *User* to the remote ftp server. If password or account is required by the remote server, they can be specified here.

ftp Command	Action
account [Password]	Send a supplemental password
bye	End ftp session and command
close	Close connection with remote host but continue ftp command
disconnect	Same as **close**
open HostName [Port]	Establish connection with remote host **HostName**, optionally on port **Port**
quit	End ftp session and command
sendport	Allow **Port** command or not
user User [Password] [Account]	Identify **User** to remote host optionally with password **Password** and account **Account**

Table 15.4. ftp commands to manage user login and password.

Managing the Characteristics of Files

Some commands enable the user to manage the characteristics of files being transferred. These commands are summarized in Table 15.5.

- **ascii** sets the file transfer type to network ASCII.

- **binary** sets the file transfer type to binary image.

- **cr** strips carriage return character from a carriage return and linefeed sequence when receiving records during ASCII-type file transfers. This option is useful when transferring files from a DOS system to a UNIX system.

- **form** specifies form of the file transfer and the only form available is file.

- **mode** sets file transfer mode but the only mode available is stream.

- **struct** sets data transfer structure type and the only available structure is stream.

- **tenex** sets file transfer type to that needed by TENEX machines.

- **type [Type]** sets file transfer type to *Type;* choices are ascii or binary.

ftp Command	Action
ascii	Sets transfer type to ASCII
binary	Sets transfer type to binary
cr	Strips carriage returns from a carriage return and line feed sequence (or not)
form	Sets **form** of file transfer
mode	Sets **mode** of file transfer
struct	Sets **structure** of file transfer
tenex	Sets transfer type to TENEX
type [Type]	Sets transfer type to **Type**

Table 15.5. **ftp** commands to manage the characteristics of files.

Miscellaneous Commands

Some commands do not fall into any easily definable category. They are described below and listed in Table 15.6.

ftp Command	Action
bell	Sounds a bell after transfer is complete
! [Command] [Parameters]	Exits to shell and optionally executes command **Command** with parameters **Parameters**
? [Subcommand]	Displays help or help on subcommand **Subcommand**
debug	Displays each command sent to host (or not)
hash	Prints a # for each 1024 bytes transferred (or not)
help	Displays information on commands
macdef	Defines a subcommand macro
modtime	Displays modification time of file on remote host
prompt	Prompts interactively (or not)
proxy [Subcommand]	Executes command on a secondary connection
remotehelp [Subcommand]	Displays help on command on remote host
reset	Clears reply queue
status	Displays status of **ftp** command
system	Displays type of system remote host is
trace	Traces packets (or not)
verbose	Displays responses from remote host (or not)

Table 15.6. ftp commands for miscellaneous tasks.

- **bell** sounds a bell after each file transfer is completed.

- **! [Command] [Parameters]** invokes an interactive shell on the local host and will execute *Command* if it is specified with *Parameters* if they are specified.

- **? [Subcommand]** displays a description of *Subcommand* or a list of available subcommands if *Subcommand* is not specified.

- **debug** toggles whether each command that is sent to the remote host will be printed (on is the default).

- **hash** toggles whether one hash sign (#) will be printed for each 1024 bytes that are transferred.

- **help** displays help information.

- **macdef** defines a subcommand macro.

- **modtime Filename** displays the last modification time of file **Filename** on the remote system.

- **prompt** toggles interactive prompting. If interactive prompting is on (the default), the **ftp** command will prompt before retrieving, sending, or deleting multiple files during **mget**, **mput**, and **mdelete** subcommands.

- **proxy [Subcommand]** executes an **ftp** command on a second control connection. Thus this command can be used to establish a connection to a second remote host to enable transferring files between the two remote hosts. The first command that should be executed under a "proxy" account should be an **open** subcommand. A list of **proxy** subcommands can be gotten by executing a **proxy ?** subcommand.

- **remotehelp [Subcommand]** requests help from the remote ftp server. If *Subcommand* is specified, only information about that subcommand will be displayed; otherwise a list of commands (at the minimum) will be displayed.

- **reset** clears the reply queue and resynchronizes the command parsing.

- **status** displays the current status of **ftp** command. For example, when you are connected to another machine and enter the command **status** you would get the response

Connected to nic.ddn.mil.
No proxy connection.
Mode: stream; Type: ascii; Form: non-print; Structure: file
Verbose: on; Bell: off; Prompting: on; Globbing: on
Store unique: off; Receive unique: off

Case: off; CR stripping: on
Ntrans: off
Nmap: off
Hash mark printing: off; Use of PORT cmds: on
Experimental commands: off

- **system** shows the type of operating system on the remote system. For example, if you are connected to another UNIX machine, you might get a response of

  215 UNIX Type: L8 Version: BSD-44

- **trace** toggles packet tracing.

- **verbose** toggles verbose mode (default is on), which will display all responses from a remote server.

Command Line Arguments for the ftp Command

Some options for the **ftp** command that can be specified by subcommands can also be specified via command line arguments. For example, the name of the host that the **ftp** command is to connect to can be specified in an **open** subcommand and can also be specified on the command line. For example, the command

ftp TestHost

will cause the **ftp** command to establish a connection with the host TestHost. Command line arguments are summarized in Table 15.7.

Displaying output that could be used for debugging problems that can be enabled by issuing the **debug** subcommand can be enabled by including the **-d** option on the command line. Disabling expansion of metacharacters in file names can be controlled by the **glob** subcommand and also by specifying the **-g** option on the command line. Disabling interactive prompting during multiple file transfers can also be controlled by the **prompt** subcommand and also by specifying the **-i** option on the command line. Specifying the **-v** option on the command line will display all the responses from the remote server and provide data transfer statistics. Normally this is the default mode but if output is being redirected to a file, the verbose mode is not in effect unless the -v option or the **verbose** subcommand is used.

Finally, one last option that is controlled by a command line argument: if the user needs to suppress automatic logging in of the user on the remote system, the user can specify the -n option on the command line. This option is needed if the user wishes to connect to another host and perform file transfers under a different user id. (See the example on "Anonymous FTP Session" later in this chapter.)

ftp Command Line Option	Action
-d	Debug mode
-g	Disable filename expansion
-i	Disable interactive prompting during file transfers
-n	Suppress automatic logging into remote system
-v	Verbose mode

Table 15.7. ftp command line options.

Some Examples of Use of the ftp Command

If you just issue the ftp command by itself, as in

ftp

the reply will be

ftp>

If you need assistance remembering what commands are available, you can enter **help** or **?** and you will have displayed on your terminal the following:

Commands may be abbreviated. Commands are:

!	delete	mdelete	proxy	runique
$	debug	mdir	sendport	send
account	dir	mget	put	size
append	disconnect	mkdir	pwd	status
ascii	form	mls	quit	struct
bell	get	mode	quote	sunique
binary	glob	modtime	recv	system
bye	hash	mput	remotehelp	tenex
case	help	nmap	rstatus	trace
cd	image	nlist	rhelp	type
cdup	lcd	ntrans	rename	user
close	ls	open	reset	verbose
cr	macdef	prompt	rmdir	?

Then an ftp prompt would again be displayed. The next command you would normally enter is **open host1** to connect to *host1*. After you entered your user id and password, you would be ready to do file operations.

If the user wanted to specify the name of the host to connect to on the command line, they would give the command

ftp nic.ddn.mil

which would attempt to connect to the host named *nic.ddn.mil*. If the connection is successful, a message such as:

Connected to nic.ddn.mil.

will appear. The ftp server on the remote host will usually send back a set of opening messages such as:

```
220-*****Welcome to the Network Information Center*****
       *****Login with username "anonymous" and password
       "guest"
       *****You may change directories to the following:
       ddn-news        - DDN Management Bulletins
       domain          - Root Domain Zone Files
       iesg            - IETF Steering Group
       ietf            - Internet Engineering Task Force
       internet-drafts - Internet Drafts
       netinfo         - NIC Information Files
       netprog         - Guest Software (ex. whois.c)
```

> *protocols   - TCP-IP & OSI Documents*
> *rfc   - RFC Repository*
> *scc   - DDN Security Bulletins*
> *std   - Internet Protocol Standards*
> *220 And more!*

Finally the ftp server on that host will ask for your name with the message

> *Name (nic.ddn.mil:fred):*

to which the user would answer with his name. For a login as a guest, you would answer

> *anonymous.*

(See a later section in this chapter for a discussion of what facilities ftp provides for public access to a system.) The remote ftp server would then prompt you for a password with the messages

> *331 Guest login ok, send "guest" as password.*
> *Password:*

You would then reply with the appropriate password, which for a public access would be *guest*. If this login sequence is accepted, the remote ftp server would give the message

> *230 Guest login ok, access restrictions apply.*

Now the user is ready to transfer files. First the user might want to change to a directory where the files of interest are and ask for a list of the files in that directory:

> **cd netprog**
> **ls**

to which the ftp server would reply with a list of files:

> *200 PORT command successful.*
> *150 Opening ASCII mode data connection for file list.*
> *whois.c.old*
> *whois.c*
> *nicusr.fai*
> *nicname.c*
> *00netprog-index.txt*
> *dns-software.txt*
> *226 Transfer complete.*

Then the local ftp client would again display the ftp prompt *ftp>*. If the user wanted to transfer the file *00netprog-index.txt*, he would enter the command

get 00netprog-index.txt

and the replies would be

200 PORT command successful.
150 Opening ASCII mode data connection for 00netprog-index.txt (567 bytes).
226 Transfer complete.
578 bytes received in 0.2343 seconds (2.409 Kbytes/s)

and the ftp prompt would be displayed indicating that another command could be entered. Figure 15.1 is the dialogue that would ensue if the user wanted to transfer two files *fyi-index.txt* and *rfc-index.txt* from the *../rfc* directory. After the user has transferred the files of interest and wants to end the session, he or she would enter the command **quit** and the connection would be ended.

---

ftp> **cd ../rfc**
250 CWD command successful.
ftp> **get fyi-index.txt**
200 PORT command successful.
150 Opening ASCII mode data connection for fyi-index.txt (5867 bytes).
226 Transfer complete.
5996 bytes received in 0.1843 seconds (31.78 Kbytes/s)
ftp> **ls *index*.***
200 PORT command successful.
150 Opening ASCII mode data connection for file list.
fyi-index.txt
rfc-index.txt
226 Transfer complete.
ftp> **get rfc-index.txt**
200 PORT command successful.
150 Opening ASCII mode data connection for rfc-index.txt (168866 bytes).
226 Transfer complete.
173092 bytes received in 7.725 seconds (21.88 Kbytes/s) ftp>

Figure 15.1. Dialogue during an **ftp** transfer of two files.

As discussed earlier in this chapter, it is possible to set up a file (*.netrc*) so that a user can automatically log into another host. With this capability it is possible to build scripts of commands to transfer files without user intervention. Another possibility is to turn off automatically logging in and provide the name of the user and the password in the set of commands that are read in by the **ftp** command. Figure 15.2 is an example of a C shell script to transfer two files (*fyi-index.txt* and *rfc-index.txt*) and to transfer an RFC (*rfcNN.txt*) if NN is specified on the command line. As an example, if the script is call **ftp_comm** and command that is entered on the command line is

> **ftp_comm 1349**

the output that is generated is shown in Figure 15.3, which shows the user *anonymous* with password *guest* logging in on the host *nic.ddn.mil* and then retrieving three files, *fyi-index.txt, rfc-index.txt,* and *rfc1349.txt.*

```
#!/bin/csh -f
#
#       Parameter is number of RFC file to retrieve
#
echo "user anonymous guest" >> /tmp/$$M
echo "cd rfc" >> /tmp/$$M
echo "get fyi-index.txt" >> /tmp/$$M
echo "get rfc-index.txt" >> /tmp/$$M
if ($#argv > 1) echo "get rfc$1.txt" >> /tmp/$$M
echo "quit" >> /tmp/$$M
ftp -nv nic.ddn.mil < /tmp/$$M >& ftp.out
rm /tmp/$$M
#
```

Figure 15.2. C shell script to transfer files.

Connected to nic.ddn.mil.
220-*****Welcome to the Network Information Center*****
*****Login with username "anonymous" and password "guest"
*   *****You may change directories to the following:*
*   ddn-news   - DDN Management Bulletins*
*   domain   - Root Domain Zone Files*
*   ~ (output removed)*
rfc   - RFC Repository
220 And more!
331 Guest login ok, send "guest" as password.
230 Guest login ok, access restrictions apply.
250 CWD command successful.
200 PORT command successful.
150 Opening ASCII mode data connection for fyi-index.txt
*   (5867 bytes).*
226 Transfer complete.
5996 bytes received in 0.4014 seconds (14.59 Kbytes/s)
200 PORT command successful.
150 Opening ASCII mode data connection for rfc-index.txt
*   (168866 bytes).*
226 Transfer complete.
173092 bytes received in 8.203 seconds (20.61 Kbytes/s)
200 PORT command successful.
150 Opening ASCII mode data connection for rfc1349.txt
*   (68949 bytes).*
226 Transfer complete.
70573 bytes received in 2.937 seconds (23.46 Kbytes/s)
221 Goodbye.

Figure 15.3. Dialogue during file transfer using C shell script.

Another ftp Example: "Anonymous" File Transfer

When using the **ftp** command and connecting to a host, the user is required to provide a user id and a password. Thus for a user to have access to a host, that user has to be defined on that system and a password set up for that user on that system. But suppose a group of people want to make a set of files available to the computing public on a particular host in their facility? If they had to define every user and provide a password for every user, they would not be very willing. Instead the **ftp** command provides a special user id called *anonymous*, which will accept any password and thus provides access by every user to all files that are in the HOME directory of the *ftp* user. Then to make files available to any user that uses this method to connect to your system, you would put the files that are "public" in that directory (or in a subdirectory in that directory).

An example of a login as a guest is shown earlier in Figure 15.3 using a C shell script. An example of an interactive login as a guest is shown in Figure 15.4. While connected as the *anonymous* user, all of the directories and files in the HOME directory of the *anonymous* user are available to retrieve files from or to put files into.

---

rusty:/rusty/big/martya/rfc[1]% **ftp nic.ddn.mil**
Connected to nic.ddn.mil.
220-*****Welcome to the Network Information Center*****
*   *****Login with username "anonymous" and password "guest"*
*   *****You may change directories to the following:*
ddn-news	*- DDN Management Bulletins*
domain	*- Root Domain Zone Files*
iesg	*- IETF Steering Group*
ietf	*- Internet Engineering Task Force*
internet-drafts	*- Internet Drafts*
netinfo	*- NIC Information Files*
netprog	*- Guest Software (ex. whois.c)*
protocols	*- TCP-IP & OSI Documents*
rfc	*- RFC Repository*
scc	*- DDN Security Bulletins*
std	*- Internet Protocol Standards*

220 And more!
Name (nic.ddn.mil:martya): **anonymous**
331 Guest login ok, send "guest" as password.
Password: **guest**
230 Guest login ok, access restrictions apply.

Figure 15.4. Connecting as a "guest" for file transfers.

While the ftp server provides the ability of a user to access this host using *anonymous* as its user id, the local system administrator must set up the directories and files of *ftp's* HOME directory to have the appropriate permissions.

What ftp Reply Messages Mean

ftp commands are interactive in that every command will be followed by at least one line of reply message. Sometimes there will be several reply messages while the operation proceeds, but every command is followed by at least one reply.

Replies to an **ftp** command have a particular format: the first field in the reply is a three-digit number called the reply code, followed by either a space or a minus sign, and then some text. The reply codes are designed to be read and analyzed by a process and thus follow a particular format. The first digit of the reply as listed in Table 15.8 indicates how the request is being performed while the second digit of the reply code indicates what kind of error it is, as shown in Table 15.9.

After the reply code, there will be at least one line of text for human beings to read. If more than one line of reply is necessary, a minus sign in the first message line signals the existence of multiple lines of reply and the final line of reply begins with the error code. A full list of ftp reply codes is shown in Table 15.10.

Leading Digit in ftp Reply Codes	Meaning of Message
1yz	Positive Preliminary Reply
2yz	Positive Completion Reply
3yz	Positive Intermediate Reply
4yz	Transient Negative Completion Reply
5yz	Permanent Negative Completion Reply

Table 15.8. Meaning of leading digit in **ftp** reply codes.

Middle Digit in ftp Reply Codes	Meaning of Message
x0z	Syntax errors
x1z	Informational Message
x2z	Connection Message
x3z	Authentication and Accounting Message
x4z	Not Currently Used
x5z	File System Messages

Table 15.9. Meaning of middle digit in **ftp** reply codes.

Code	Meaning of Message
110	Restart marker reply. In this case, the text is exact and not left to the particular implementation; it must read: 　　　MARK yyyy = mmmm Where yyyy is User-process data stream marker, and mmmm server's equivalent marker (note the spaces between markers and "=").
120	Service ready in nnn minutes.
125	Data connection already open; transfer starting.
150	File status okay; about to open data connection.
200	Command okay.
202	Command not implemented, superfluous at this site.
211	System status, or system help reply.
212	Directory status.
213	File status.
214	Help message. On how to use the server or the meaning of a particular nonstandard command. This reply is useful only to the human user.
215	NAME system type. Where NAME is an official system name from the list in the Assigned Numbers document.

Table 15.10. ftp reply codes in numeric order.

Code	Meaning of Message
220	Service ready for new user.
221	Service closing control connection. Logged out if appropriate.
225	Data connection open; no transfer in progress.
226	Closing data connection. Requested file action successful (for example, file transfer or file abort).
227	Entering Passive Mode (h1,h2,h3,h4,p1,p2).
230	User logged in, proceed.
250	Requested file action okay, completed.
257	"PATHNAME" created.
331	User name okay, need password.
332	Need account for login.
350	Requested file action pending further information.
421	Service not available, closing control connection. This may be a reply to any command if the service knows it must shut down.
425	Can't open data connection.
426	Connection closed; transfer aborted.
450	Requested file action not taken. File unavailable (e.g., file busy).
451	Requested action aborted: local error in processing.
452	Requested action not taken. Insufficient storage space in system.
500	Syntax error, command unrecognized. This may include errors such as command line too long.
501	Syntax error in parameters or arguments.
502	Command not implemented.
503	Bad sequence of commands.
504	Command not implemented for that parameter.
530	Not logged in.
532	Need account for storing files.
550	Requested action not taken. File unavailable (e.g., file not found, no access).
551	Requested action aborted: page type unknown.
552	Requested file action aborted. Exceeded storage allocation (for current directory or dataset).
553	Requested action not taken. File name not allowed.

Table 15.10. ftp reply codes in numeric order. (cont'd)

How the ftp Server Functions

Ftp commands and replies are exchanged through one connection, while data is transferred over a separate connection, as shown in Figure 15.5. The FTP Client communicates with the FTP Server on the remote host using TCP as the intermediary protocol, as shown in Figure 15.6. The ftp Connection Protocol follows the telnet Protocol methodology. During transfers, the status of the data transfers can be determined at any time because separate connections are used. Even if the data transfer is aborted, the other connection allows status information to be exchanged. Thus the connection for data transfer is temporary and transient.

All ftp commands are displayed with a reply message in mind. Thus at any point in an ftp session the state of the user will be known. For example, sending the message "int" puts that user into the "waiting for reply" state, and when the reply is received and finished the user will be in the "waiting to send command" state.

Some commands will cause more than one reply from the server but since the reply messages are coded, the user can determine whether to expect another reply message. For the command "retrieve file", the first reply is a "Positive Preliminary Reply" (100), indicating that the command is accepted and being processed and other messages can be expected.

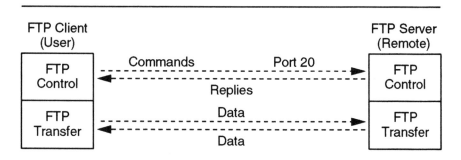

Figure 15.5. ftp client/server interaction.

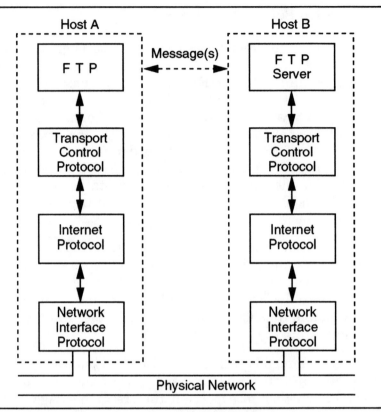

Figure 15.6. ftp interaction with other TCP/IP protocols.

Summary

The **ftp** command is used to transfer file between the local host and a remote host or between two remote hosts. Options can be specified to ensure that transferred files have unique file names. The names of files can be manipulated so that the naming conventions of the receiving host can be followed. Scripts can be created that will perform the file transfers for the user. Public access to files is provided via the "anonymous" login.

The standard TCP/IP File Transfer facilities and how they function are described in RFC 959, "File Transfer Protocol," written by J. Postel and J. Reynolds in 1985. For further information on the **ftp** command itself, examine the manual pages on the UNIX system of interest.

16

Electronic Mail Services

Introduction

One service that users desire is to be able to exchange messages with other users somewhere in the network. To make matters easier, users want to send a message to another user without knowing where that user is in the network. UNIX systems provide at least one basic command called **mail** to send mail to another user and to read mail. The command **mail** will be discussed in the first part of this chapter.

The hosts can be on different networks, but how do they set up the messages so that they can be delivered to the user on the system that is intended? Typical mail addresses are two-level: the first level is the name of the user, and the second level is the name of the host using network names. The operation that enables mail to be delivered to another user is invisible to the user.

TCP/IP provides a protocol to exchange mail between users called Simple Mail Transfer Protocol (SMTP). The functionality of SMTP is designed to deliver mail reliably. SMTP is designed to work with any reliable byte stream and can be used on top of protocols other than TCP.

How to Send Mail to Another User

Messages can be sent to another user using the **mail** command. For example, the command

mail john

will start the "mail editor" to build a message for the user named *john* and, when you have finished composing the message, will send that message to the user named *john*. The name of the user is sufficient to identify to whom the message is to be sent if the user is locally defined. If the user is not locally defined, the address of the user must be included in the format

john@company1.com

which indicates that the user "john" is known to the host named *company1.com*. Thus to send a message to someone not on your system, you must know the host on which that user is defined.

Input to the **mail** command can be provided by a file, as in the command

mail john@company1.com < letter_to_john

which will send *john@company1.com* the contents of the file *letter_to_john*. If the user wants to add the subject to the mail message, add the *-s* option, as in the command

mail -s Greetings john@company1.com

which will send *john@company1.com* a message with the subject "Greetings". If more than one user is to receive a message, a list of users can be specified instead of just one user.

The **mail** command is also used to read the messages that have been sent to a user. Entering the **mail** command without any other arguments will be responded to with a list of unread mail messages.

How the sendmail Server Functions

The **sendmail** server moves messages (that is to say, "mail") from one host to another with the goal being to move the message to the host on which the user resides. To assist sendmail in this noble task, aliases are defined that inform the sendmail server which users are defined on this host. Other messages received by the sendmail server will be moved on to another host that is known to be able to deliver the message to the user to which it is addressed.

Some Examples of Use of sendmail Services

The **sendmail** server can be queried to determine whether the sendmail server knows the address of the users defined on the remote host. To check out how various users are defined, a user connects to the sendmail server and queries the sendmail server to determine which users the sendmail server knows about. Users can connect to the sendmail server by using the **telnet** command to attach to the remote host of interest with the well-known port of the sendmail server. For example, if the user enters the command

telnet RemoteHost 25

the sendmail server will respond

Trying...
Connected to RemoteHost.company1.com.
Escape character is '^]'.
220 company1.com 5.65c/IDA-1.4.4 Sendmail is ready at Mon,
14 Sep 1992 21:37:26 -0400

Once the connection to the sendmail server is established, the requesting host should identify itself, as in the following:

helo Local.Company1.com

and the sendmail server will acknowledge the requesting host with the reply

250 Hello Local.Company1.com, pleased to meet you

If the user incorrectly identifies the local host, the sendmail server will respond

250 Hello Local.What.com why do you call yourself Local?

The following command can be used to query whether the sendmail server knows about a particular user:

vrfy User1

and the sendmail server will respond with the full name of the user asked about if it knows the user's name, or with the message "550 User1... User unknown" if the user is not known.

If the user wants to know what commands are defined, the user would enter the **help** command, and the reply will be

```
214-Commands:
214-   HELO    MAIL    RCPT  DATA  RSET
214-   NOOP    QUIT    HELP  VRFY  EXPN
214-For more info use "HELP <topic>".
214-To report bugs in the implementation contact
sendmail@okeeffe.Berkeley.EDU
214-For local information contact postmaster at this site.
214 End of HELP info
```

If the user wants to determine the contents of a mailing list, the user would use the **expn** command. If the mailing list exists, the sendmail server will respond with the names of the users on that mailing list.

How Mail Gets Transferred From One Host to Another

SMTP defines a set of commands with strict syntax that are used to move mail messages from one host to another. These functions are not user-visible. To set up mail systems requiring addresses of users there is usually another command on the system; for AIX it would be sendmail. The **sendmail** command will set up aliases and mail addresses so that mail can be sent from one user to another.

SMTP delivers mail by establishing a transmission path between an SMTP client (in the literature, this is called a "Sender-SMTP") and an SMTP server on a remote host (in the literature, a "Receiver-SMTP"). Once this pathway is established, the SMTP client sends a message to the SMTP server indicating who the recipient of the mail is (using an SMTP RCPT command). If the SMTP server can accept mail addressed to that user, it will reply with an OK reply; if it cannot, it will reject that recipient. This type of negotiation will proceed for several recipients until the SMTP client has exhausted its list of recipients for which it has mail.

Once the list of recipients has been agreed upon, the SMTP client transmits the mail messages to the SMTP server (using MAIL commands).

SMTP has been implemented in a manner that is independent of the transport protocol used. For TCP/IP-based networks, TCP is used as the transport mechanism, as illustrated in Figure 16.1.

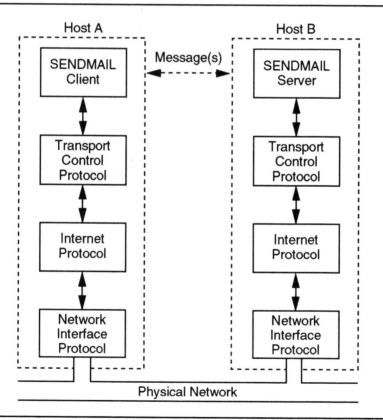

Figure 16.1. SMTP client/server interaction with protocols.

In order to enable the relaying of mail messages from one host to another and then to another, the MAIL commands all contain the fully qualified name of the user that the mail is from (usually called the "reverse-path"), while the RCPT commands all contain the fully qualified name of the user to whom the mail is being sent (usually called the "forward-path"). In this way, SMTP clients/servers can become aware of how to relay mail from one user to another even when they are not on the same network.

The various commands that SMTP uses are summarized in Table 16.1. Commands and replies to commands are not case-sensitive, but the forward-path and reverse-path may be. User names are case-sensitive on some UNIX platforms while host names are not case-sensitive. Each of the commands in Table 16.1 must be on a line by itself and that line must be ended by carriage return and linefeed.

Replies are three-digit numbers; the left digit indicates the type of reply or pattern. A list of all the possible reply codes and their meaning is shown in Table 16.2.

Some hosts provide the service of delivering mail directly to a user's terminal. SMTP provides compatibility with this method of operation by defining commands that implement "sending". Delivery of mail to a mailbox is considered to be "mailing". To support this, the various forms of the SEND command replace the MAIL command in the interaction between the SMTP client and SMTP server.

Summary

The **mail** command is usually described in a manual page on your UNIX system. In addition, there are a number of mail-reading programs, some commercially available, which provide a number of services to make the reading and writing of mail messages easier. These will usually be described in their own manual pages.

The protocol for a mail services server is described in RFC 821, "Simple Mail Transfer Protocol," written by Jonathan B. Postel, August 1982. A companion text, "Standard for the Format of ARPA Internet Text Messages" (RFC 822), describes how message addresses should be formatted so that mail servers can understand them and can deliver the mail properly.

Mail Command	Meaning of Mail Command
MAIL FROM: *<reverse-path>*	Tells SMTP server that the SMTP client has mail from *<reverse-path>*
RCPT TO: *<forward-path>*	Tells SMTP server that the SMTP client has mail for the user named in *<forward-path>*
DATA	Tells SMTP server that the next lines are message text until a line is received that contains only a period (.), which indicates the end of message text
VRFY *<user name>*	Asks SMTP server to indicate the full name of the user. If the full user name is not known, a reply "User not local" will be sent back. If this is a mailing list and not a single user, a reply "User ambiguous" will be sent back.
EXPN *<mailing list>*	Asks SMTP server to indicate what users are on this mailing list
SEND FROM: *<reverse-path>*	Asks the mail message to be delivered to a user's terminal
SOML FROM: *<reverse-path>*	Asks the mail message to be delivered to a user's terminal if the user is active or to the user's mailbox if the user is not active
SAML FROM: *<reverse-path>*	Asks the mail message to be delivered to a user's terminal if the user is active and also to the user's mailbox
HELO *<domain>*	Tells the SMTP server what the name of the SMTP client is
QUIT	Tells the SMTP server that the transmission is over
TURN	SMTP server must send an OK reply and assume the role of the SMTP client

Table 16.1. Simple Mail Transfer Protocol commands.

CODE	Meaning of Reply Code
211	System status, or system help reply
214	Help message [Information on how to use the receiver or the meaning of a particular nonstandard command; this reply is useful only to the human user]
220	<domain> Service ready
221	<domain> Service closing transmission channel
250	Requested mail action okay, completed
251	User not local; will forward to <forward-path>
354	Start mail input; end with <CRLF>.<CRLF>
421	<domain> Service not available, closing transmission channel [This may be a reply to any command if the service knows it must shut down]
450	Requested mail action not taken: mailbox unavailable [for example, mailbox busy]
451	Requested action aborted: local error in processing
452	Requested action not taken: insufficient system storage
500	Syntax error, command unrecognized [This may include errors such as command line too long]
501	Syntax error in parameters or arguments
502	Command not implemented
503	Bad sequence of commands
504	Command parameter not implemented
550	Requested action not taken: mailbox unavailable [for example, mailbox not found, no access]
551	User not local; please try <forward-path>
552	Requested mail action aborted: exceeded storage allocation
553	Requested action not taken: mailbox name not allowed [for example, mailbox syntax incorrect]
554	Transaction failed

Table 16.2. SMTP reply codes in numeric order.

17

Accessing Remote
Files Locally

Introduction

Files that physically reside on a remote host can seem to be locally
available in the sense that local operations can be performed on
them, such as editing them or using them in a program that is
executing on the local host. Making remote files locally available
is effected by using Network file services to create "Network File
Systems." The original work in this area was done by Sun
Microsystems. Currently these services are not a part of the "standard" TCP/IP suite but there are a number of proposals to "stan-
dardize" the network file services and add them to the TCP/IP
Protocol suite. This chapter will describe what the network file
services can do and how this is accomplished.

How to Use the Network File
Services (mount) Command

Network file services can be invoked by the user by executing
the **mount** command, which asks that file systems on a remote
host be made available on the local host for users to access
locally. These file systems may be local (actually physically
attached to the local host) or they may be remote (that is,
physically attached to a remote host). The **mount** command

requires that the user know which is the case, but once the **mount** command is successful this distinction will not be visible. The mount command is

> **mount RemoteHost1:/goodstuff /goodstuff**

which is a request to mount a directory on *RemoteHost1* called */goodstuff* as */goodstuff*. Usually remote file systems are mounted on a local system using the identical name as the remote file system. A remote file system can be mounted on a local system under a name different from its name on the remote system, but users can be confused by this approach. Once a file system is successfully mounted, changing to the */goodstuff* directory on the local system will make available to the local user the same files that a user on the remote system sees.

A user can determine if a file is on the local host or on the remote host by using the **df** command or by examining the permissions attributes of the file. The **df** command is simply

> **df /happy/large**

which requests information about the directory */happy/large*. The information may look like

```
Filesystem    Total KB    used      free     %used   Mounted on
happy:/large  1247180   1077308   169872    86%    /happy/large
```

which indicates that the directory */happy/large* is actually on a remote host named *happy*. Often remote file systems are named using the name of the remote host as the top-level directory name, but this is not required. If the user executes the command

> **ls -l /happy**

the display would be

> Drwxrwxrwx 32 root adm 1024 Sep 17 18:01 large/

and for the command

> **ls -l /happy/large**

the display would be

Frw-r——	1 marty	adm	7600	Sep 10	15:26	acaca.prtx
Drwxr-xr-x	2 marty	adm	512	Jul 07	16:02	about/
Frwxr-xr-x	1 marty	adm	9922	Aug 31	16:50	backup.out*
Drwxr-xr-x	2 marty	adm	512	Aug 18	17:31	config/
Drwxr-xr-x	2 marty	adm	512	Jul 09	16:12	convert/
Frwxr-xr-x	˙2 marty	adm	4434	Sep 11	16:12	commit*
Frw-r——	1 marty	adm	13927	Aug 31	14:21	database

where the capital letters F (to designate a file) and D (to designate a directory) indicate that these are remotely located files and directories. Unfortunately, not every version of UNIX marks remote files this way; some versions do not change the permissions on a remote file.

To obtain a list of the file systems available on a host, the user would use the **df** command. As an example, a display of the various file systems on a particular host is displayed in Figure 17.1. For this system there were two file systems from the host *jerico* plus one system each from the hosts *happy, goofy, and sleepy.* (The file systems called */dev/hdX* are local file systems.) Note that it is not necessary that the directory name on the remote host be the same as the directory name on the local host. For practical reasons, system administrators generally include the name of the remote host in the name by which the local host knows that file system.

Filesystem	Total KB	used	free	%used	Mounted on
/dev/hd4	53248	42388	10860	79%	/
/dev/hd2	253952	249224	4728	98%	/usr
/dev/hd9var	4096	1980	2116	48%	/var
/dev/hd3	8192	1188	7004	14%	/tmp
jerico:/usr/local	262144	232752	29392	88%	/usr/local
jerico:/u	49152	44280	4872	90%	/u
happy:/large	1247180	1077308	169872	86%	/happy/large
goofy:/usr/local2	81548	63572	17976	77%	/usr/local2
sleepy:/good	524280	33744	490536	6%	/good

Figure 17.1. Sample output from **df** command.

For most systems, both local and remote file systems can be described in a special file called *filesystems,* which is usually in the */etc* directory. Each entry in this file will describe a file system indicating its location, name of directory in that location, and the name of the directory it is to be known as on the local host. Some sample entries from such a file are shown in Figure 17.2.

```
/usr/local:
        dev             = /usr/local
        vfs             = nfs
        nodename        = jerico
        mount           = true
        check           = false
        type            = nfs
        options         = bg,rsize=1024,wsize=1024
/happy/large:
        dev             = /large
        vfs             = nfs
        nodename        = happy
        mount           = true
        check           = false
        type            = nfs
        options         = bg,hard,intr,rsize=1024,wsize=1024
/usr/local2:
        dev             = /usr/local2
        vfs             = nfs
        nodename        = goofy
        mount           = true
        check           = false
        type            = nfs
        options         = bg,hard,intr,rsize=1024,wsize=1024
```

Figure 17.2. Sample entries in */etc/filesystems* file.

Summary

This chapter has described how file systems on remote hosts can be made available on local hosts without copying any files using Network File System functions.

Manual pages describe the **mount** command and the **df** command. Three RFCs form the basic documentation of how the Network File Systems operate: RFC 1094 describes the overall approach to Network File Systems; RFC 1050 describes the Remote Procedure Calls that are used by the Network File Systems' clients and servers; and RFC 1014 describes how data that is managed by the network file services is encoded.

18

Miscellaneous Network Services

Introduction

A number of services may be offered as part of a TCP/IP-based network. These services are optional but, if they are offered, they must follow a defined standard protocol. Several of these services are useful in diagnosing network problems. These optional services are listed in Table 18.1. Each of these services is described in this chapter.

Network Service	Port	What Service Does
Echo	7	Sends back to requestor any transmitted message
Discard	9	Discards all messages that it receives
Character Generator	19	Sends back to requestor all of the possible printable ASCII characters
Time	37	Sends back to requestor time in seconds since midnight, January 1, 1900
Daytime	13	Sends back to requestor the date and time including day of the week, month of the year
Active Users	11	Sends back to requestor which users are active on remote system
Quote of the Day	17	Sends back to requestor a quote of the day

Table 18.1. Miscellaneous TCP/IP network services.

How Echo Network Service Functions

The Echo service will send back to the originating application any data it receives. The echo service can operate as either a connection-based TCP service or a connectionless UDP service. As a connection service, the echo server listens on TCP port 7 for TCP connection requests. Once the connection is established, any data that is received is sent back to the originating application. The echoing of messages will continue until the connection is broken. An echo server also listens on UDP port 7 for datagrams. When a datagram is received, the data in it is sent back to the originating source. Since the data that is received is just sent back to the originating application, the performance of the network could be tested by measuring the time that it takes for the data to arrive at the remote host and be transmitted back. This turnaround time will measure the response time and latency in the network connection between the host and the remote host to which it is connected.

How Discard Network Service Functions

The Discard service discards any data that is sent to it. The discard service operates both as a TCP connection-based service and as a UDP-based connectionless service. As a TCP service, a server will listen on TCP port 9 for connections and, when a connection is established, will discard any data sent to it without reporting an error or sending back a response. As a UDP service, a server will listen on UDP port 9 for datagrams and will discard any datagrams it receives without any error and without sending a response.

How Character Generator Network Service Functions

The Character Generator service simply sends character data of a prescribed format to any source that connects to it or sends a datagram to it. Any input that is sent to it will be ignored. The TCP character generator service listens on TCP port 19 for TCP connection. Once a connection is established, the input is discarded and a stream of character data in a particular pattern is sent to the originating source. Data will continue to be sent until the connection is broken. Users may abort the connection at any time. The normal TCP data flow mechanism will keep the character-generating process from sending the user data faster than it can process it. The UDP character generator service listens for datagrams on UDP port 19. When a datagram is received, a datagram is sent to the originating source that contains a random number (between 0 and 512) of characters. One popular pattern for the character data to be sent is a 72-character line of ASCII characters, generated from the 95 printable ASCII characters. Such a pattern is illustrated in Figure 18.1. The set of 72 characters that is sent is rotated so that eventually all 95 ASCII characters have been sent. Thus you can test the ability of a printer to print all the ASCII characters and the ability of the network to transmit properly all 95 ASCII characters.

```
!"#$%&'()*+,-./0123456789:;<=>?@ABCDEFGHIJKLMNOPQRSTUVWXYZ[\]^_`abcdefg
!"#$%&'()*+,-./0123456789:;<=>?@ABCDEFGHIJKLMNOPQRSTUVWXYZ[\]^_`abcdefgh
"#$%&'()*+,-./0123456789:;<=>?@ABCDEFGHIJKLMNOPQRSTUVWXYZ[\]^_`abcdefghi
#$%&'()*+,-./0123456789:;<=>?@ABCDEFGHIJKLMNOPQRSTUVWXYZ[\]^_`abcdefghij
$%&'()*+,-./0123456789:;<=>?@ABCDEFGHIJKLMNOPQRSTUVWXYZ[\]^_`abcdefghijk
%&'()*+,-./0123456789:;<=>?@ABCDEFGHIJKLMNOPQRSTUVWXYZ[\]^_`abcdefghijkl
&'()*+,-./0123456789:;<=>?@ABCDEFGHIJKLMNOPQRSTUVWXYZ[\]^_`abcdefghijklm
'()*+,-./0123456789:;<=>?@ABCDEFGHIJKLMNOPQRSTUVWXYZ[\]^_`abcdefghijklmn
()*+,-./0123456789:;<=>?@ABCDEFGHIJKLMNOPQRSTUVWXYZ[\]^_`abcdefghijklmno
)*+,-./0123456789:;<=>?@ABCDEFGHIJKLMNOPQRSTUVWXYZ[\]^_`abcdefghijklmnop
*+,-./0123456789:;<=>?@ABCDEFGHIJKLMNOPQRSTUVWXYZ[\]^_`abcdefghijklmnopq
+,-./0123456789:;<=>?@ABCDEFGHIJKLMNOPQRSTUVWXYZ[\]^_`abcdefghijklmnopqr
,-./0123456789:;<=>?@ABCDEFGHIJKLMNOPQRSTUVWXYZ[\]^_`abcdefghijklmnopqrs
-./0123456789:;<=>?@ABCDEFGHIJKLMNOPQRSTUVWXYZ[\]^_`abcdefghijklmnopqrst
./0123456789:;<=>?@ABCDEFGHIJKLMNOPQRSTUVWXYZ[\]^_`abcdefghijklmnopqrst
0123456789:;<=>?@ABCDEFGHIJKLMNOPQRSTUVWXYZ[\]^_`abcdefghijklmnopqrstu
123456789:;<=>?@ABCDEFGHIJKLMNOPQRSTUVWXYZ[\]^_`abcdefghijklmnopqrstuv
123456789:;<=>?@ABCDEFGHIJKLMNOPQRSTUVWXYZ[\]^_`abcdefghijklmnopqrstuvw
23456789:;<=>?@ABCDEFGHIJKLMNOPQRSTUVWXYZ[\]^_`abcdefghijklmnopqrstuvw
3456789:;<=>?@ABCDEFGHIJKLMNOPQRSTUVWXYZ[\]^_`abcdefghijklmnopqrstuvwx
456789:;<=>?@ABCDEFGHIJKLMNOPQRSTUVWXYZ[\]^_`abcdefghijklmnopqrstuvwxy
56789:;<=>?@ABCDEFGHIJKLMNOPQRSTUVWXYZ[\]^_`abcdefghijklmnopqrstuvwxyz
6789:;<=>?@ABCDEFGHIJKLMNOPQRSTUVWXYZ[\]^_`abcdefghijklmnopqrstuvwxyz{l
789:;<=>?@ABCDEFGHIJKLMNOPQRSTUVWXYZ[\]^_`abcdefghijklmnopqrstuvwxyz{l}
89:;<=>?@ABCDEFGHIJKLMNOPQRSTUVWXYZ[\]^_`abcdefghijklmnopqrstuvwxyz{l}~
```

Figure 18.1. Output from Character Generator network service.

How Time Network Service Functions

The Time service sends back to the originating source the time in seconds since midnight, January 1, 1900. This type of service is used to synchronize time on a set of hosts. The TCP time service listens on TCP port 37 and, when a connection is established, will send the current time and then close the connection. The UDP time service listens on UDP port 37 and, when a datagram is received, will respond with the current time as a 32-bit binary number.

How Daytime Network Service Functions

The Daytime service sends back to the originating source the date and time in the format: day of the week, month of the year, day of the month, time in HH:MM:SS, and the year, with these fields separated by blanks. The TCP Daytime Service listens on TCP port 13 and, when a connection is established, will respond with the date and time and then close the connection. The UDP daytime service listens on UDP port 13 and, when a datagram is received, will respond with the date and time as the remote host knows it.

How Active Users Network Service Functions

The Active Users service will send back to the originating source a list of the users currently active on the host. The TCP active users service listens on port 11 and, when a connection is established, will respond with a list of the currently active users and then close the connection. The UDP active users service listens on UDP port 11 and, when a datagram is received, will respond with a list of users.

How Quote of the Day Network Service Functions

The Quote of the Day service will send back to the requesting source a quote of the day when requested.

How to Use the Miscellaneous Network Services

Each of the miscellaneous network services are used by establishing a connection with the appropriate TCP port for that service or by sending a UDP datagram to the UDP port of interest.

One method for using these services is to use **telnet** to establish a TCP connection with the port that offers the services of interest. For example, the command

telnet hoşta 7

will establish a connection to the *echo* service of *hosta* (if it is running). Now when you type in any characters and touch the return key, those characters will be echoed back to you on your terminal. Such a telnet session might look like the following:

```
Trying...
    Connected to kwhiz.kronos.com.
    Escape character is '^T'.
sssss<return>
sssss
sssssssss<return>
sssssssss
jjkkll<return>
jjkkll
^T
```

But if instead of the *echo* service, the *discard* service is connected to with the telnet command **telnet hosta 9**, the above telnet session might look like

```
Trying...
    Connected to kwhiz.kronos.com.
    Escape character is '^T'.
sssss<return>
sssssssss<return>
jjkkll<return>
^T
```

where no response is received from the remote host *hosta* but no error is signaled either, and the connection is continued for as long as is wished.

As another example, the command

telnet hosta 19

will establish a connection to the *character generator* service on host *hosta*. This connection will cause a stream of characters such as shown in Figure 18.1 to be displayed on your terminal until you abort the connection.

As another example, the command

telnet hosta 13

will establish a connection to the *daytime* service on host *hosta*. The output from that command will be displayed on your terminal and will look like

Trying...
Connected to hosta.companyname.com.
Escape character is '^T'.
Mon Aug 10 22:30:54 1992
Connection closed.

which indicates that a standard telnet connection is established long enough for the date and time to be sent from the remote host *hosta* and then the connection is closed. This type of command could be used to determine the date and time on a set of computers in a network and ensure that they all have the same date and time.

Summary

A variety of miscellaneous network services can be available to be used as network test tools or to enable a standard date and time on every host throughout the network. One service will echo back to the source host any data it is sent. Another service will send to the requesting host output that contains all of the printable ASCII characters. Another service will return to the requesting host a list of users currently active on that host.

Each of the miscellaneous network services is described in a separate RFC. Table 18.2 lists the RFC that is the basis for each of the services. For further study of any of these services, users can examine the appropriate RFC.

Network Service	RFC
Echo	862
Discard	863
Character Generator	864
Quote of the Day	865
Time	868
Daytime	867
Active Users	866

Table 18.2. RFCs describing miscellaneous network services.

Appendix A:
TCP/IP Standards
Documents

What TCP/IP Standards Documents Exist

The TCP/IP standards are currently being overseen by the Internet Architecture Board (IAB), which is a group of networking users who banded together to organize a worldwide network called the "Internet." This group is responsible for assigning network addresses and for specifying the protocols that can be used in the Internet. The number of users of the Internet has exploded in the last few years, creating an enormous internetwork that is worldwide.

The Internet Architecture Board has chosen to publish its protocol standards in a format called Request For Comments, or RFCs. These RFCs cover a variety of topics and may not be intended to be used as standards documents but rather as discussion documents. The number that an RFC has is assigned as soon as it is requested by the author of the soon-to-be-published RFC. RFCs often undergo editing as they are discussed but, as soon as they are formally issued, no further modification of the RFC will occur. In addition, RFC numbers are not reused. But if new information on a subject needs to be added to an old RFC, the subject can be reused under a new RFC. For example, one particular RFC called "Assigned Numbers" has been issued a number of times as more specifications of TCP/IP values has been added to the RFC.

All of this RFC activity can be confusing because a user will want to read the latest RFC on a subject but how does the user find out which RFC is the latest for that subject?

Two master documents exist that provide an overall guide to the available RFCs and their subjects. The names of the files that these two documents are: *fyi-index.txt*, which provides a running commentary on what RFC activities are occurring; *rfc-index.txt*, which lists all the RFCs and their subject and, in particular, indicates which RFC obsoletes which previously issued RFC. These two documents are available from the same sources that the other RFCs are and probably should be read first. The next document to read is the RFC that has *IAB Official Protocol Standards* as its subject. This document contains a discussion of how the TCP/IP Protocol standards process works and the current status of the various standards documents. As an example, this document will list which RFC has the latest list of "Assigned Numbers," which RFC describes the File Transfer Protocol, and so forth.

Finally, there are the RFCs themselves. Some of the RFCs are detailed specifications of the various protocols that have been accepted as part of the TCP/IP Protocol suite. In addition, there are RFCs that are discussions of various network-related topics, and there are even RFCs that are poetry or just commentary on network life.

Tables A.1 through A.4 list the various RFCs that have been written to specify the standards that the Internet Authorization Board has accepted (as of January 1, 1993). For each RFC there is shown both a Status and a State. A shorthand analysis of what the States and Statuses mean is illustrated in Table A.5. The State of a protocol indicates its maturity. Protocols labeled "std" are part of the set of standard protocols, while the other States indicate the level of discussion and acceptance of a proposed protocol. For example, examining Table A.1 of Standard Protocols, it can be seen that protocols such as IP and ICMP are required as part of any implementation of TCP/IP Protocols while protocols such as DISCARD or ECHO are optional and can be chosen to be implemented. Protocols such as TCP, UDP, and so forth are in the category where an implementation of TCP/IP should contain them.

The Status of a protocol indicates how an implementation of TCP/IP should treat these standards.

Protocol	Name	State	Status	RFC(S)
———	IAB Official Protocol Standards	Std	Req	1360
———	Assigned Numbers	Std	Req	1340
———	Host Requirements — Communications	Std	Req	1122
———	Host Requirements — Applications	Std	Req	1123
———	Gateway Requirements	Std	Req	1009
IP	Internet Protocol	Std	Req	791
	as amended by:———			
———	IP Subnet Extension	Std	Req	950
———	IP Broadcast Datagrams	Std	Req	919
———	IP Broadcast Datagrams w/ Subnets	Std	Req	922
ICMP	Internet Control Message Protocol	Std	Req	792
IGMP	Internet Group Multicast Protocol	Std	Rec	1112
UDP	User Datagram Protocol	Std	Rec	768
TCP	Transmission Control Protocol	Std	Rec	793
TELNET	Telnet Protocol	Std	Rec	854,855
FTP	File Transfer Protocol	Std	Rec	959
SMTP	Simple Mail Transfer Protocol	Std	Rec	821
MAIL	Format of Electronic Mail Messages	Std	Rec	822
CONTENT	Content Type Header Field	Std	Rec	1049
NTP	Network Time Protocol	Std	Rec	1119
DOMAIN	Domain Name System	Std	Rec	1034,1035
DNS-MX	Mail Routing and the Domain System	Std	Rec	974
SNMP	Simple Network Management Protocol	Std	Rec	1157
SMI	Structure of Management Information	Std	Rec	1155
MIB-II	Management Information Base—II	Std	Rec	1213
EGP	Exterior Gateway Protocol	Std	Rec	904
NETBIOS	NetBIOS Service Protocols	Std	Ele	1001,1002
ECHO	Echo Protocol	Std	Rec	862
DISCARD	Discard Protocol	Std	Ele	863
CHARGEN	Character Generator Protocol	Std	Ele	864
QUOTE	Quote of the Day Protocol	Std	Ele	865
USERS	Active Users Protocol	Std	Ele	866
DAYTIME	Daytime Protocol	Std	Ele	867
TIME	Time Server Protocol	Std	Ele	868
TFTP	Trivial File Transfer Protocol	Std	Ele	1350
RIP	Routing Information Protocol	Std	Ele	1058

Table A.1. Standard protocols as specified by Internet Architecture Board.

Protocol	Name	State	Status	RFC
IP-FR	Multiprotocol over Frame Relay	Prop	Ele	1294
IP-SMDS	Transmission of IP Datagrams over SMDS	Prop	Ele	1209
ARP	Address Resolution Protocol	Std	Ele	826
RARP	Reverse Address Resolution Protocol	Std	Ele	903
IP-ARPA	Internet Protocol on ARPANET	Std	Ele	BBN1822
IP-WB	Internet Protocol on Wideband Network	Std	Ele	907
IP-X25	Internet Protocol on X.25 Networks	Std	Ele	877
IP-E	Internet Protocol on Ethernet Networks	Std	Ele	894
IP-EE	Internet Protocol on Exp. Ethernet Nets	Std	Ele	895
IP-IEEE	Internet Protocol on IEEE 802	Std	Ele	1042
IP-DC	Internet Protocol on DC Networks	Std	Ele	891
IP-HC	Internet Protocol on Hyperchannel	Std	Ele	1044
IP-ARC	Internet Protocol on ARCNET	Std	Ele	1051
IP-SLIP	Transmission of IP over Serial Lines	Std	Ele	1055
IP-NETBIOS	Transmission of IP over NETBIOS	Std	Ele	1088
IP-IPX	Transmission of 802.2 over IPX Netwrks	Std	Ele	1132
IP-FDDI	Transmission of IP over FDDI	Draft	Ele	1188

Table A.2. Network-specific standard protocols as specified by Internet Architecture Board.

Protocol	Name	State	Status	RFC(S)
FINGER	Finger Protocol	Ele	Draft	1288
BGP3	Border Gateway Protocol 3 (BGP-3)	Ele	Draft	1267,1268
OSPF2	Open Shortest Path First Routing V2	Ele	Draft	1247
POP3	Post Office Protocol, Version 3	Ele	Draft	1225
Concise-MIB	Concise MIB Definitions	Ele	Draft	1212
IP-FDDI	Internet Protocol on FDDI Networks	Ele	Draft	1188
TOPT-LINE	Telnet Linemode Option	Ele	Draft	1184
PPP	Point to Point Protocol	Ele	Draft	1171
BOOTP	Bootstrap Protocol	Rec	Draft	951,1084
TP-TCP	ISO Transport Service on top of TCP	Ele	Draft	1006
NICNAME	WhoIs Protocol	Ele	Draft	954

Table A.3. Draft standard protocols as specified by Internet Architecture Board.

Protocol	Name	State	Status	RFC
TOPT-BIN	Binary Transmission	Std	Rec	856
TOPT-ECHO	Echo	Std	Rec	857
TOPT-RECN	Reconnection	Prop	Ele	...
TOPT-SUPP	Suppress Go Ahead	Std	Rec	858
TOPT-APRX	Approx Message Size Negotiation	Prop	Ele	...
TOPT-STAT	Status	Std	Rec	859
TOPT-TIM	Timing Mark	Std	Rec	860
TOPT-REM	Remote Controlled Trans and Echo	Prop	Ele	726
TOPT-OLW	Output Line Width	Prop	Ele	...
TOPT-OPS	Output Page Size	Prop	Ele	...
TOPT-OCRD	Output Carriage-Return Disposition	Prop	Ele	652
TOPT-OHT	Output Horizontal Tabstops	Prop	Ele	653
TOPT-OHTD	Output Horizontal Tab Disposition	Prop	Ele	654
TOPT-OFD	Output Formfeed Disposition	Prop	Ele	655
TOPT-OVT	Output Vertical Tabstops	Prop	Ele	656
TOPT-OVTD	Output Vertical Tab Disposition	Prop	Ele	657
TOPT-OLD	Output Linefeed Disposition	Prop	Ele	658
TOPT-EXT	Extended ASCII	Prop	Ele	698
TOPT-LOGO	Logout	Prop	Ele	727
TOPT-BYTE	Byte Macro	Prop	Ele	735
TOPT-DATA	Data Entry Terminal	Prop	Ele	1043
TOPT-SUP	SUPDUP	Prop	Ele	734
TOPT-SUPO	SUPDUP Output	Prop	Ele	749
TOPT-SNDL	Send Location	Prop	Ele	779
TOPT-TERM	Terminal Type	Prop	Ele	1091
TOPT-EOR	End of Record	Prop	Ele	885
TOPT-TACACS	TACACS User Identification	Prop	Ele	927
TOPT-OM	Output Marking	Prop	Ele	933
TOPT-TLN	Terminal Location Number	Prop	Ele	946
TOPT-3270	Telnet 3270 Regime	Prop	Ele	1041
TOPT-X.3	X.3 PAD	Prop	Ele	1053
TOPT-NAWS	Negotiate About Window Size	Prop	Ele	1073
TOPT-TS	Terminal Speed	Prop	Ele	1079
TOPT-RFC	Remote Flow Control	Prop	Ele	1080
TOPT-LINE	Linemode	Draft	Ele	1184
TOPT-XDL	X Display Location	Prop	Ele	1096
TOPT-EXTOP	Extended Options List	Std	Rec	861

Table A.4.   Telnet option protocols as specified by Internet Architecture Board.

Status	Meaning
Req	Required Protocol; must be implemented
Rec	Recommended Protocol; should be implemented
Ele	Elective Protocol; may be implemented
Lim	Limited Use Protocol; may be implemented
NotRec	Not Recommended Protocol; don't implement

State	Meaning
Std	Standard Protocol
Draft	Draft Standard Protocol; possible future standard protocol; being tested; revision of Draft Standard possible
Prop	Proposed Standard Protocol; considered for future Standard Protocol; being tested by limited groups; revision of Proposed Standard expected
Exp	Experimental Protocol; being used for testing purposes only
Info	Informational Protocol; protocols developed by other organizations, may be recommended for use in the Internet
Hist	Historical Protocol; Unlikely to ever become standard

Table A.5. Various Statuses and States an RFC can have.

How to Get TCP/IP Standards Documents

RFCs can be obtained from a number of network sources, but the source for those sources is *nic.ddn.mil*. At this location is all of the RFCs plus many of the discussion documents that are circulated before an RFC is issued. RFCs are available from *nic.ddn.mil via* "anonymous" ftp through the internet. If a user connects to *nic.ddn.mil* and then lists the directories that are available, the following will be displayed on the terminal:

```
200 PORT command successful.
  150 Opening ASCII mode data connection for file list.
  lost+found
```

```
netinfo
bin
ietf
dev
ien
iso
scc
ddn-news
etc
home
protocols
rfc
usr
isode
tcp-ip
netinfo:
std
internet-drafts
fyi
templates
ddn-news:
iesg
domain
namedroppers
pub
demo
netprog
226 Transfer complete.
```

If the user changes to the rfc directory using the **cd rfc** and executes the **ls** command, a list of all the available RFCs will be displayed in the format rfc*nnnn*.txt where *nnnn* is the number of the RFC:

```
200 PORT command successful.
150 Opening ASCII mode data connection for file list.
rfc-by-author.txt
rfc-by-title.txt
rfc-index.txt
rfc10.txt
rfc1000.txt
rfc1001.txt
rfc1002.txt
```

> *rfc1003.txt*
> *rfc1004.txt*
> *(etc.)*

In addition, two other documents are available (rfc-by-author.txt and rfc-by-title.txt), which list by author or title which RFCs are available. To examine RFC 834, the user would use the **get** command:

get rfc834.txt

and RFC 834 would be transferred to the local host.

Many other lists are available from *nic.ddn.mil*. For example, if instead of looking for an RFC the user is looking for a list of the current defined hosts in the internet, the user would change to the *domain* subdirectory to display the following list of files:

```
150 Opening ASCII mode data connection for /bin/ls.
total 2417
-rw-rw-rw-  1  64          2486  Sep 15  05:13 arpa.zone
-rw-rw-rw-  1  64        870167  Sep 15  19:56 com.zone
-rw-rw-rw-  1  64        205062  Sep 15  20:07 edu.zone
-rw-rw-rw-  1  64         32899  Sep 15  05:18 gov.zone
-rw-rw-rw-  1  64       1027745  Sep 15  05:33 inaddr.zone
-rw-rw-rw-  1  64        145468  Sep 15  20:12 mil.zone
-rw-rw-rw-  1  64         29884  Sep 15  20:08 net.zone
-rw-rw-rw-  1  64         74834  Sep 15  20:09 org.zone
-rw-rw-rw-  1  64         28853  Sep 15  05:12 root.zone
226 Transfer complete.
```

Thus for each type of host on the internet, there is a list of currently connected hosts. Each of these lists can be retrieved from the remote host in the usual way.

Appendix B: Glossary of Networking Terms

Many terms are peculiar to networking. This appendix contains acronyms and shorthand ways to refer to various objects that have to do with networking and TCP/IP. Other terms have been added as well.

ASCII: American Standard Code for Information Interchange. The ASCII character set is as defined in the ARPA-Internet Protocol Handbook. In FTP, ASCII characters are defined to be the lower half of an 8-bit code set (i.e., the most significant bit is zero). In more general terms ASCII is defined by America Standards Institute, X3.4, 1968.

address mask: A bit mask used to select bits from an Internet address for subnet addressing. The mask is 32 bits long and selects the network portion of the Internet address and one or more bits of the local portion. Sometimes called subnet mask.

address resolution: A means for mapping network layer addresses onto media-specific addresses. See *ARP*.

ANSI: American National Standards Institute. The U.S. standardization body. ANSI is a member of the International Organization for Standardization (ISO).

API: Application Program Interface. A set of calling conventions defining how a service is invoked through a software package.

application layer: The topmost layer in the TCP/IP model providing such communication services as electronic mail, file transfer, and remote terminal connection.

ARP: Address Resolution Protocol. The Internet protocol used to dynamically map Internet addresses to physical (hardware) addresses on local area networks. Limited to networks that support hardware broadcast.

ARPA: Advanced Research Projects Agency; now called DARPA. The U.S. government agency that funded the ARPANET. See *DARPA*.

ARPANET: A packet-switched network developed in the early 1970s. The "grandfather" of today's Internet. ARPANET was decommissioned in June 1990.

autonomous system: Internet (TCP/IP) terminology for a collection of gateways (routers) that fall under one administrative entity and cooperate using a common Interior Gateway Protocol (IGP). See *subnetwork*.

backbone: The primary connectivity mechanism of a hierarchical distributed system. All systems that have connectivity to an intermediate system on the backbone are assured of connectivity to each other. This does not prevent systems from setting up private arrangements with each other to bypass the backbone for reasons of cost, performance, or security.

baseband: Characteristic of any network technology that uses a single-carrier frequency and requires all stations attached to the network to participate in every transmission. See *broadband*.

bridge: A node, connected to two or more administratively indistinguishable but physically distinct subnets, that automatically forwards datagrams when necessary but whose existence is not known to other hosts. Bridges can usually be made to filter packets, that is, to forward only certain traffic. Also called a "software repeater." See *repeater, router.*

broadband: Characteristic of any network that multiplexes multiple, independent network carriers onto a single cable. This is usually done using frequency division multiplexing. Broadband technology allows several networks to coexist on one single cable; traffic from one network does not interfere with traffic from another since the "conversations" happen on different frequencies in the "ether," rather like the commercial radio system.

broadcast: A packet delivery system where a copy of a given packet is given to all hosts attached to the network. Example: Ethernet.

BSD: Berkeley Software Distribution. Term used when describing different versions of the Berkeley UNIX software, as in "4.3BSD UNIX."

catenet: A network in which hosts are connected to networks with varying characteristics, and the networks are interconnected by gateways (routers). The Internet is an example of a catenet.

CCITT: International Consultative Committee for Telegraphy and Telephony. A unit of the International Telecommunications Union (ITU) of the United Nations. An organization with representatives from the PTTs of the world. CCITT produces technical standards, known as "Recommendations," for all internationally controlled aspects of analog and digital communications.

client: A process that requests services from another process, usually called a "server." See *server.*

client-server model: A common way to describe network services and the model user processes (programs) of those services. Examples include the name-server/name-resolver paradigm of the Domain Name System and file-server/file-client relationships such as NFS and diskless hosts. See *NFS.*

connectionless: The model of interconnection in which communication takes place without first establishing a connection. Sometimes (imprecisely) called datagram. Examples: LANs, Internet IP, UDP, ordinary postcards.

connection-oriented: The model of interconnection in which communication proceeds through three well-defined phases: connection establishment, data transfer, and connection release. Examples: X.25, Internet TCP, ordinary telephone calls.

CSMA/CD: Carrier Sense Multiple Access with Collision Detection. The access method used by local area networking technologies such as Ethernet.

daemon: Process that runs continuously in the background, waiting for some event to occur or some condition to be true. Daemons are the original method of providing services in a UNIX system. Most servers are daemons.

DARPA: Defense Advanced Research Projects Agency. The U.S. government agency that funded the ARPANET.

Data Link Layer: The OSI layer that is responsible for data transfer across a single physical connection, or series of bridged connections, between two network entities.

destination The destination address, an internet header field.

DNS: Domain Name System. The distributed name/address mechanism used in the Internet.

domain: In the Internet, a part of a naming hierarchy. Syntactically, an Internet domain name consists of names (labels) separated by periods (dots), e.g., "tundra.mpk.ca.us."

dotted decimal notation: The syntactic representation of a 32-bit integer that consists of four 8-bit numbers written in base 10 with periods (dots) separating them. Used to represent IP addresses in the Internet, such as: 192.67.67.20.

EGP: Exterior Gateway Protocol. A reachability routing protocol used by gateways in a two-level internet. EGP is used in the Internet core system. See *core gateway*.

encapsulation: The technique used by layered protocols in which a layer adds header information to the data from the layer above. As an example, in Internet terminology a packet would contain a header from the physical layer, followed by a header from the network layer (IP), followed by a header from the transport layer (TCP), followed by the Application Protocol data.

end system: A system that contains application processes capable of communicating through all seven layers of TCP/IP protocols. Equivalent to Internet host.

entity: OSI terminology for a layer protocol machine. An entity within a layer performs the functions of the layer within a single computer system, accessing the layer entity below and providing services to the layer entity above at local service access points.

Ethernet: A widely used local area network technology invented at the Xerox Corporation Palo Alto Research Center. Medium is passive coaxial cable and uses CSMA/CD access technology.

fragmentation: The process in which an IP datagram is broken into smaller pieces to fit the requirements of a given physical network. The reverse process is termed reassembly. See *MTU*.

frame: A frame is the unit of transmission in a data link layer protocol, and consists of a data link layer header followed by a packet.

FTP: File Transfer Protocol. The Internet protocol (and program) used to transfer files between hosts.

gateway: A node connected to two or more administratively distinct networks and/or subnets, to which hosts send datagrams to be forwarded. The original Internet term for what is now called router, or more precisely, IP router. In modern usage, the terms "gateway" and "application gateway" refer to systems that do translation from some native format to another. Examples include X.400 to/from RFC 822 electronic mail gateways. See *router*.

header: Control information at the beginning of a message, segment, datagram, packet, or block of data.

host: A computer in the internetwork environment on which mailboxes or SMTP processes reside.

IAB: Internet Activities Board. The technical body that oversees the development of the Internet suite of protocols (commonly referred to as "TCP/IP"). It has two task forces (the IRTF and the IETF), each charged with investigating a particular area.

ICMP: Internet Control Message Protocol. The protocol used to handle errors and control messages at the IP layer. ICMP is used from gateways to hosts and between hosts to report errors and make routing suggestions. ICMP is actually part of the IP protocol.

IESG: Internet Engineering Steering Group. The executive committee of the IETF.

IETF: Internet Engineering Task Force. One of the task forces of the IAB. The IETF is responsible for solving short-term engineering needs of the Internet. It has over 40 Working Groups.

IGP: Interior Gateway Protocol. The protocol used to exchange routing information between collaborating routers in the Internet. RIP and OSPF are examples of IGPs.

intermediate system: A system that is not an end system, but that serves instead to relay communications between end systems. See *repeater, bridge, router*.

internet: A collection of networks interconnected by a set of routers that allow them to function as a single, large virtual network.

Internet (note the capital "I"): The largest internet in the world, consisting of large national backbone nets (such as MILNET, NSFNET, and CREN) and a myriad of regional and local campus networks all over the world. The Internet uses the Internet Protocol suite. To be on the Internet you must have IP connectivity, i.e., be able to Telnet to— or ping—other systems. Networks with only e-mail connectivity are not actually classified as being on the Internet.

internet address: A 32-bit address assigned to hosts using TCP/IP. A source or destination address consisting of a Network field and a Local Address field and possibly a Subnet Number field. See *dotted decimal notation*.

internet datagram: The unit of data exchanged between a pair of internet modules (includes the internet header).

internet fragment: A portion of the data of an internet datagram with an internet header.

IP: Internet Protocol. The network layer protocol for the Internet Protocol suite.

IP datagram: The fundamental unit of information passed across the Internet and the unit of end-to-end transmission in IP protocol that contains source and destination addresses, along with data and a number of fields that define such things as the length of the datagram, the header check sum, and flags to say whether the datagram can be (or has been) fragmented.

IRTF: Internet Research Task Force. One of the task forces of the IAB. The group responsible for research and development of the Internet Protocol suite.

ISDN: Integrated Services Digital Network. An emerging technology that is beginning to be offered by the telephone carriers of the world. ISDN combines voice and digital network services in a single medium, making it possible to offer customers digital data services as well as voice connections through a single "wire." The standards that define ISDN are specified by CCITT.

ISO: International Organization for Standardization is an international standards group best known for the seven-layer OSI Reference Model. See *OSI*.

Local address: The address of a host within a network. The actual mapping of an internet local address onto the host addresses in a network is quite general, allowing for many-to-one mappings.

mail gateway: A machine that connects two or more electronic mail systems (especially dissimilar mail systems on two different networks) and transfers messages between them. Sometimes the mapping and translation can be quite complex, and generally it requires a store-and-forward scheme whereby the message is received from one system completely before it is transmitted to the next system after suitable translations.

message: The unit of transmission in a transport layer protocol. In particular, a TCP segment is a message. A message consists of a transport protocol header followed by application protocol data. To be transmitted end-to-end through the Internet, a message must be encapsulated inside a datagram. This term is used by some application layer protocols (particularly SMTP) for an application data unit.

MTU: Maximum Transmission Unit. The largest possible unit of data that can be sent on a given physical medium. Example: The MTU of Ethernet is 1500 bytes. See *fragmentation*.

multicast: A special form of broadcast where copies of the packet are delivered to only a subset of all possible destinations. See *broadcast*.

multi-homed host: A computer connected to more than one physical data link. The data links may or may not be attached to the same network. A host is said to be multi-homed if it has multiple IP addresses.

name resolution: The process of mapping a name into the corresponding address. See *DNS*.

NetBIOS: Network Basic Input Output System. The standard interface to networks on IBM PC and compatible systems.

network layer: The OSI layer that is responsible for routing, switching, and subnetwork access across the entire OSI environment.

NFS(R): Network File System. A distributed file system developed by Sun Microsystems that allows a set of computers to cooperatively access each other's files in a transparent manner.

NIC: Network Information Center. Originally there was only one, located at SRI International and tasked to serve the ARPANET (and later DDN) community. Today, there are many NICs of local, regional, and national networks all over the world. Such centers provide user assistance, document service, training, and much more.

node: A computer in the internetwork environment on which internet protocol services are available.

octet: An 8-bit byte.

OSI: Open Systems Interconnection. An international standardization program to facilitate communications among computers from different manufacturers. See *ISO*.

OSPF: Open Shortest Path First. A "Proposed Standard" IGP for the Internet. See *IGP*.

packet: A packet is the unit of data passed across the interface between the internet layer and the link layer. It includes an IP header and data. A packet may be a complete IP datagram or a fragment of an IP datagram.

path: The sequence of gateways such that, at a given moment, all the IP datagrams going from a particular source host to a particular destination host will traverse. A path is unidirectional; it is not unusual to have different paths in the two directions between a given host pair.

PDU: Protocol Data Unit. This is OSI terminology for "packet." A PDU is a data object exchanged by protocol machines (entities) within a given layer. PDUs consist of both Protocol Control Information (PCI) and user data.

physical layer: The OSI layer that provides the means to activate and use physical connections for bit transmission. In plain terms, the physical layer provides the procedures for transferring a single bit across a physical media.

physical media: Any means in the physical world for transferring signals between OSI systems. Considered to be outside the OSI Reference Model, and therefore sometimes referred to as "Layer 0." The physical connector to the media can be considered as defining the bottom interface of the physical layer, i.e., the bottom of the OSI Reference Model.

physical network interface: This is a physical interface to a connected network and has a (possibly unique) link-layer address. Multiple physical network interfaces on a single host may share the same link-layer address, but the address must be unique for different hosts on the same physical network.

ping: Packet internet groper. A program used to test reachability of destinations by sending them an ICMP echo request and waiting for a reply. The term is used as a verb: "Ping host X to see if it is up!"

port: The entity on a host that performs as a logical network communications channel and is used by Internet transport protocols to distinguish among multiple simultaneous connections to a single destination host. Part of the full address of a particular application on a particular port. A particular port on a host can be addressed by a client to request a particular service. Port numbers are assigned for the standard set of services, called "well-known" ports.

PPP: Point-to-Point Protocol. The successor to SLIP, PPP provides router-to-router and host-to-network connections over both synchronous and asynchronous circuits. See *SLIP*.

presentation layer: The OSI layer that determines how application information is represented (i.e., encoded) while in transit between two end systems.

protocol: A formal description of messages to be exchanged and rules to be followed for two or more systems to exchange information.

proxy: The mechanism whereby one system "fronts for" another system in responding to protocol requests. Proxy systems are used in network management to avoid having to implement full protocol stacks in simple devices such as modems.

proxy ARP: The technique in which one machine, usually a router, answers ARP requests intended for another machine. By "faking" its identity, the router accepts responsibility for routing packets to the "real" destination. Proxy ARP allows a site to use a single IP address with two physical networks. Subnetting would normally be a better solution.

RARP: Reverse Address Resolution Protocol. The Internet protocol a diskless host uses to find its Internet address at startup. RARP maps a physical (hardware) address to an Internet address. See *ARP*

repeater: A device that propagates electrical signals from one cable to another without making routing decisions or providing packet filtering. In OSI terminology, a repeater is a physical layer intermediate system. See *bridge, router.*

RFC: Request For Comments. The document series, begun in 1969, that describes the Internet suite of protocols and related experiments. Not all (in fact, very few) RFCs describe Internet standards, but all Internet standards are written up as RFCs.

RFS: Remote File System. A distributed file system, similar to NFS, developed by AT&T and distributed with their UNIX System V operating system. See *NFS.*

RIP: Routing Information Protocol. An Interior Gateway Protocol (IGP) supplied with Berkeley UNIX.

rlogin: A service offered by Berkeley UNIX that allows users of one machine to login to other UNIX systems (for which they are authorized) and interact as if their terminals were connected directly. Similar to *Telnet.*

router: A system responsible for making decisions about which of several paths network or internetwork traffic will follow. To do this it uses a routing protocol to gain information about the network, and a set of algorithms to choose the best route based on several criteria known as "routing metrics." In OSI terminology, a router is a network layer intermediate system. See *gateway, bridge, repeater.*

RPC: Remote Procedure Call. An easy and popular paradigm for implementing the client-server model of distributed computing. A request is sent to a remote system to execute a designated procedure, using arguments supplied, and the result returned to the caller. There are many variations and subtleties, resulting in a variety of different RPC protocols.

segment: A segment is the unit of end-to-end transmission in the TCP Protocol. A segment consists of a TCP header followed by application data. A segment is transmitted by encapsulation inside an IP datagram.

server: The entity that provides services when it is requested by a client. Servers are usually daemons on a UNIX system. See *client-server model*, *daemon*.

session: The set of transactions that are exchanged while the transmission channel is open.

session layer: The OSI layer that provides the pathway for dialogue control between end systems.

SLIP: Serial Line IP. An Internet protocol used to run IP over serial lines such as telephone circuits or RS-232C cables interconnecting two systems. SLIP is now being replaced by PPP. See *PPP*.

SMI: Structure of Management Information. The rules used to define the objects that can be accessed via a network management protocol. See *MIB*.

SMTP: Simple Mail Transfer Protocol. The Internet electronic mail protocol. Defined in RFC 821, with associated message format descriptions given in RFC 822.

SNMP: Simple Network Management Protocol. The network management protocol of choice for TCP/IP-based internets.

source: The source address, an internet header field.

subnet: A single member of the collection of hardware networks that compose an IP network. Host addresses on a given subnet share an IP network number with hosts on all other subnets of that IP network, but the local-address part is divided into subnet-number and hostnumber fields to indicate which subnet a host is on. A particular division of the local-address part is not assumed; this could vary from network to network.

Subnet field: The bit field in an Internet address denoting the subnet number. The bits making up this field are not necessarily contiguous in the address.

subnet mask: The designation of which bits in the internet dotted-decimal scheme of addresses form the subnet number. See *address mask*.

subnetwork: A collection of end systems and intermediate systems under the control of a single administrative domain and utilizing a single network access protocol. Examples: private X.25 networks, collection of bridged LANs.

subnet number: A number identifying a subnet within a network.

TCP: Transmission Control Protocol. The major transport protocol in the Internet suite of protocols providing reliable, connection-oriented, full-duplex streams. Uses IP for delivery.

TCP segment: The unit of data exchanged between TCP modules (including the TCP header).

Telnet: The virtual terminal protocol in the Internet suite of protocols. Allows users of one host to login to a remote host and interact as normal terminal users of that host.

TFTP: Trivial File Transfer Protocol. A simple file transfer protocol built on UDP.

transaction: The set of exchanges required for one message to be transmitted for one or more recipients.

transceiver: Transmitter-receiver. The physical device that connects a host interface to a local area network such as Ethernet. Ethernet transceivers contain electronics that apply signals to the cable and sense collisions.

transmission channel: A full-duplex communication path between a sender-SMTP and a receiver-SMTP for the exchange of commands, replies, and mail text.

transport layer: The OSI layer that is responsible for reliable end-to-end data transfer between end systems.

transport service: Any reliable stream-oriented data communication services; for example, TCP.

virtual circuit: A connection that is established between two application programs.

UDP: User Datagram Protocol. A transport protocol in the Internet suite of protocols. UDP, like TCP, uses IP for delivery; however, unlike TCP, UDP provides for exchange of datagrams without acknowledgments or guaranteed delivery.

UDP datagram: A UDP datagram is the unit of end-to-end transmission in the UDP protocol.

UUCP: UNIX to UNIX Copy Program. A protocol used for communication between consenting UNIX systems.

XDR: eXternal Data Representation. A standard for machine-independent data structures developed by Sun Microsystems. Similar to *ASN.1*.

Summary

Many of the RFCs that have been published by the IAB have extensive sections on terminology. In addition, RFC 1240 contains just terminology and acronyms used in the RFC literature. The various RFCs provide the basis for an extensive glossary of terms and acronyms.

Index